PREPARE, SUCCEED, ADVANCE

PREPARE, SUCCEED, ADVANCE

A Guidebook for Getting a PhD in Biblical Studies
and Beyond

—Second Edition—

NIJAY K. GUPTA

CASCADE *Books* · Eugene, Oregon

PREPARE, SUCCEED, ADVANCE
A Guidebook for Getting a PhD in Biblical Studies and Beyond, Second Edition

Cascade Books
An Imprint of Wipf and Stock Publishers
199 W. 8th Ave., Suite 3
Eugene, OR 97401
www.wipfandstock.com

PAPERBACK ISBN: 978-1-5326-6830-2
HARDCOVER ISBN: 978-1-5326-6831-9
EBOOK ISBN: 978-1-5326-6832-6

Cataloging-in-Publication data:

Names: Gupta, Nijay K., author.

Title: Prepare, succeed, advance : a guidebook for getting a PhD in biblical studies and beyond, second edition / by Nijay K. Gupta

Description: Eugene, OR : Cascade Books, 2019 | Includes bibliographical references.

Identifiers: ISBN 978-1-5326-6830-2 (paperback) | ISBN 978-1-5326-6831-9 (hardcover) | ISBN 978-1-5326-6832-6 (ebook)

Subjects: LCSH: Doctor of philosophy degree. | Graduate students—Handbooks, manuals, etc. | Universities and colleges—Graduate work.

Classification: LCC LB2386 G75 2019 (print) | LCC LB2386 (ebook)

Manufactured in the U.S.A.   04/26/19

Contents

Acknowledgments

At least once a month for the past several years I have received emails or messages on social media from readers of the first edition of this book, thanking me for the information and advice I provided. That has been very gratifying. But the academy continues to change and develop, and I have been learning new things about being a researcher and teacher as well, so I thought it was time for a new edition. There are at least four major updates for this edition. First, the book needed strengthening in some nuts and bolts issues, so I enlisted the help of friends who have succeeded in these areas and know the ins and outs of the current state of things: thank you Julianna Smith (who wrote a section for me on the GRE) and Marcus Jerkins (who wrote a new section on doctoral examinations). Second, I wanted to address questions about and interest in distance learning options. Third, in the last several years I have worked hard to become a better teacher, so I have added extensively to my advice on pedagogy. Finally, and perhaps most importantly, I offer a new reflection on striving towards a more inclusive and diverse biblical studies guild.

I wish to dedicate this new edition to several people who have mentored me, took a chance on me and believed in me, and/or pushed me to achieve excellence: Mrs. Linda Walther, Dr. Steve Nimis, Dr. Catherine Kroeger, Dr. Roy Ciampa, Dr. Barry Corey, Dr. Walter Kaiser, Prof. John Barclay, Dr. Stephen Barton, Dr. Jim Critchlow, Dr. Michael Gorman, Dr. Todd Still, Dr. Chris Spinks, Dr. Michael F. Bird, Prof. James D. G. Dunn, Dr. Douglas Strong, Dr. Doug Cullum, Dr. Chuck Conniry, Dr. Scot McKnight, and Dr. Roger Nam. I also wish to acknowledge my parents, Dr. Mohinder and Sudesh Gupta, and my supportive family, Amy, Simryn, Aidan, and Libby.

Introduction

When I was an undergraduate at Miami University (Ohio, not Florida), I took several business classes. It happened that the main archway of the business school building had a striking inscription etched into the brick: "Ye shall know the truth, and the truth shall make you free." Now, of course, these are Jesus' words from John 8:32, though the inscription bore no reference. I don't know exactly why these words were written on the building, but even if it was not in the name of recognizing religious truth, there is still a general maxim that fits these words: knowledge offers power. The more you know about a situation or a subject, the more options you will have. Your eyes are opened, as it were, to the wider landscape. Having a deeper knowledge of "what is out there" allows one to prepare for the future, and such preparation offers a measure of freedom to control where one ends up. I desire to offer my own experience and knowledge to others in hopes that they will be able to have the freedom to discern the best academic and professional future.

This book is one that I wish I had fifteen years ago when I first began to think seriously about pursuing a doctoral degree. It is a practical book, a nuts-and-bolts kind of resource. It was written out of a desire to demystify both the preparation for and experience of a PhD. Over the last decade, I have compiled many questions and most of their answers. I had very few people who gave me direction for how to apply to, gain entrance to, and survive a PhD program, and I hoped one day to have some answers, based on my own experience, that I could pass on to others. So, on the one hand, many will find this book useful, as it comes from my own trial-and-error experiences. On the other hand, in these pages you will find the experience of basically only one person—me. Therefore, though I draw almost exclusively from my own life, my advice has been tested by other professors and especially by other doctoral students. When I wrote the first edition of this

1

book, I was only a year out of my doctoral program. Now, I am nearing a decade in teaching and professional participation in the academy. I have the benefit of experience in nine different colleges or seminaries as a student or professor. I now supervise doctoral students (DMin), I administrate the graduate thesis program at Portland Seminary, and I serve on the doctoral faculty of Trinity College Bristol (United Kingdom).

MY JOURNEY

A very natural question to ask when perusing this book and assessing its accuracy and utility is what makes you (the author) a reliable guide? What I offer, as stated above, is subjective. Nevertheless, it is true that most people venturing into this world will have similar questions to answer, challenges to face, and obstacles to overcome academically. It might help, then, to know where I am coming from and what I have done.

I studied for my bachelor's degree at Miami University (OH), where I majored in public relations and also concentrated on classical Greek. Largely out of a love for studying Greek, I went to Gordon-Conwell Theological Seminary (MA) and received a master of divinity and master of theology with a focus on New Testament Greek and Biblical theology. During that time, I had a number of formative academic experiences, including serving as a Greek teaching assistant for a few years. The next year, I worked full-time at Hendrickson Publishers as their academic specialist for sales and marketing while teaching as an adjunct instructor for Gordon-Conwell's urban campus in Boston. It was at this time that I applied to doctoral programs in New Testament and accepted an offer to study at the University of Durham (England) with Professor John M. G. Barclay and Dr. Stephen C. Barton. I completed my PhD in 2009, and my dissertation was subsequently published with Walter de Gruyter (Berlin, Germany) under the title *Worship That Makes Sense to Paul: A New Approach to the Theology and Ethics of Paul's Cultic Metaphors*. During my PhD, I also wrote and published over a dozen journal articles (*JSNT*, *Neotestamentica*, *Journal for the Study of the Pseudepigrapha*, etc.).

Immediately following the completion of my doctorate, I held several visiting positions at places such as Ashland Theological Seminary, Seattle Pacific University and Seminary, and Eastern University, and now I serve as associate professor of New Testament at Portland Seminary. In 2017, I was voted to membership of the Society of New Testament Studies, and in 2018 I received the Faculty Achievement Award for Graduate Research and Scholarship at George Fox University/Portland Seminary. I have published three commentaries, a monograph, and coedited a Festschrift, and I serve on the editorial board of the *Journal for the Study of Paul and His Letters* and *Ex Auditu*. 2019 will see the publication of several more publications including a Pauline monograph (*Paul and the Language of Faith*), a reference work on 1–2 Thessalonians (*Zondervan Critical Introduction to the New Testament: 1–2 Thessalonians*), and an edited volume entitled *The State of New Testament Studies* (coedited with Scot McKnight). I am also on the editorial team for the planned second edition of the *Dictionary of Paul and His Letters*.

THE FOCUS AND LIMITATIONS OF THE BOOK

As the title of the book makes clear, the focus of our attention is on those interested in biblical studies. There are several reasons for this specificity. First and foremost, my own degree is in New Testament and, thus, I can write most accurately about that academic world and its processes. Furthermore, I chose to pursue my doctorate in England, even though I am an American. However, two caveats should be made. Firstly, I researched American New Testament (and Christian origins) programs intensively when I was at the stage where I was applying to doctoral programs. Though they certainly differ in many ways, and noticeably in format and length, there is still a great deal of overlap in terms of criteria for acceptance and the significance of the writing project for earning the degree. Secondly, while I cannot comment in depth regarding all fields of religious studies, my advice is, I believe, relevant in many ways to those interested in pursuing a PhD in many divisions of theological and religious studies (and especially Old Testament/Hebrew Bible research). Therefore, my hope is that this book will be accessed by and useful to more than that small group of academics who desire to pursue New Testament studies. Many issues related to choosing the right program, writing the thesis, or presenting papers at conferences are common to all researchers and students. Beyond only entering and completing a doctorate, I also offer counsel on engaging in the academic teaching world beyond the PhD, as new professors often feel lost in a world without supervisors.

SIZING UP THE CHALLENGE

There are a number of reasons why people decide to earn a doctorate in biblical studies or theology. Often, though not always, it is borne out of a faith commitment and a hunger to learn about the Bible (or doctrine) and to become prepared to teach the Bible. For others, the attraction involves a fascination with that peculiar group of people that made such an impact on world history—whether the people of Israel in the ancient Mediterranean world or the early Christians in the Greco-Roman world. Such ambitions and inspirations can be exhilarating and naturally lead to dreams of giving lectures and engaging with students, researching for books and articles, and interacting with scholars in the faculty lounge or the conference hall. I feel that it is appropriate at this point, though, to put the academic path in perspective, as I have seen some students flippantly decide to pursue a doctorate without sizing up the challenge. In the first place, it is, for almost all people—especially in an academic context—that one is praised for excelling and ignored when struggling. Therefore, one must be prepared for some tough times, as supervisors and examiners can sometimes be terse, blunt, or even boorish. But that is getting ahead of ourselves; the first hurdle is, of course, gaining entry into a good doctoral program. Many aspiring academics are unaware of how difficult it is. For instance, and we will return to this matter later, top graduate schools only admit a small handful of doctoral students in New Testament (or Old Testament) per year, and they usually make their selections from hundreds of applicants! Another factor to consider, before glibly planning out your future, is the reality of the job market. Every year, students graduate from scores of doctoral programs and compete for a relatively small number of jobs. Despite these bleak numbers, though, excellent professors and researchers in biblical studies are still needed, and some doctoral programs are thriving. I believe, nevertheless, that one should be aware of the difficult road ahead. I hope my role will be—once the decision has been made to push forward—to help you succeed in your education and vocational goals.

THE PLAN OF THE BOOK

There are basically three parts to this book that enable one to gain entrance to and survive a New Testament PhD program, as well as to advance into the professional academic world. The first part, *Prepare*, involves the work

4

that goes into selecting and successfully gaining admission to a doctoral program. The second part, *Succeed*, focuses squarely on the experience within the program and is geared towards writing a cogent and defensible dissertation.[1] These two parts are meant to lead someone to complete his or her doctoral degree successfully. However, if one is hoping to gain academic employment, usually the institution judges candidates based on factors in addition to their degree status, including teaching ability and experience, research interests, publications in periodicals, and academic service experience. Therefore, a final part will handle these matters under the rubric *Advance*. This area will also be relevant to recently hired professors as they launch their careers.

---

1. In America, the doctoral-level research project is typically called a "dissertation." In England, the same kind of project is referred to as a "thesis." For the sake of consistency, I will use "dissertation" for a doctoral project, and "thesis" for a master's project.

PREPARE

1

Choosing a Doctoral Program

Perhaps the greatest challenge for someone wanting to become a professor in biblical studies is selecting the best kind of program and institution at which to study. Furthermore, it is not only important to calculate the
various factors involved in making the decision, but also thinking through
the process and contingent issues ahead of time. Practically speaking, the
advice offered in this book may be utilized and applied more efficiently for
someone at the beginning of his or her master's degree (or, even better, during a bachelor's degree) than, for instance, at the stage of actually applying
for the doctoral program. The reason why this is the case is because certain
things can be done during one's earlier education to align more properly
with the kind of institution at which one might desire to seek admission.

In this chapter, we will discuss the key factors that one must consider
when choosing doctoral programs, the difference between the American
and British systems of education, and various ideological and philosophical
considerations that usually contribute to making the "right" decision.

THE BIG SIX FACTORS: THEOLOGICAL ORIENTATION, PRESTIGE AND DIFFICULTY, MONEY, TIME, LOCATION, AND LIBRARY

Where does one begin when selecting prospective schools for doctoral
study? There are natural places that one might turn. Some people look
at where their own undergraduate and graduate professors have studied.

Others note where students who came before them in their institution tend to go. There appears to be, though, a cluster of factors that generally weigh into the decision for most students: theological orientation, prestige and difficulty, money, time, location, and library. It is important to note, though, that the significance of the various factors vary from person to person. Indeed, some people may only take interest in a select few of these or make their decision on the basis of only one or two. But, again, working on the principle that knowledge offers decision-making empowerment, I will discuss all six factors, and I hope it will become clear what their general relevance might be, though you may decide for yourself which factors are most crucial.

Theological Orientation

There are all kinds of places where one could choose to study for a PhD. There are Baptist schools and Methodist schools. There are institutions that are consciously ecumenical or interdenominational, and there are schools that are intentionally disinterested in ecclesial distinctives and "church" matters. It is reasonable, then, to consider what your educational goals are and how significant it is (if at all) to choose an institution that shares your theological interests, challenges them, or works completely apart from a "faith" perspective. On the one hand, some students desire to study in an academic environment that trains scholars to critically engage the biblical text without presumption about doctrine and creed. Others desire to teach within their own denomination and find it desirable to study at a doctoral level within that denomination to work more deeply within and for the benefit of their own tradition. Each person must decide on his or her own academic objectives and how best to go about fulfilling them.

On a personal note, though, I would add a bit of advice that was passed down to me with regard to this matter. There is a distinct advantage to studying in a university setting versus a seminary (that has no partnering university). From an academic standpoint, the university doctoral student often has access to a wide range of other departments, their faculty, and their library resources. This would permit, if desired, the potential for cross-disciplinary engagement, as a New Testament student could interact with and benefit from departments of history, classics, philosophy, anthropology, literature, sociology, and so forth. Some seminaries, though, participate in institutional consortia where one could take courses at part-nering schools in their region.

Prestige and Difficulty

There is no getting around the fact that certain institutions are well known for academic excellence (e.g., Princeton, Cambridge, Oxford, Notre Dame, Duke). And, of course, there is a *reason* why these places bear such reputa-tions. In general, they maintain a strong commitment to offering the best education with leading scholars. Though we will later address which kinds of schools are acclaimed for their religion/biblical studies departments or programs, this factor is significant in general for more than just self-satisfaction (which is, of course, also important). When it comes to the highly competitive job market, *where* you studied matters a lot in many cases. If your doctoral institution is academically very discerning in terms of admission, and you made it through successfully, there is the prudent presumption that you have very estimable academic qualities.

The flip side to this matter of prestige is that such programs are usually rigorous, either in the difficulty of their examinations or in the standards for the dissertation or both. It probably seems like an obvious decision to shoot for the most prestigious program. However, there may be reasons why this may be unnecessary. For instance, if someone was teaching at a small institution with only a master's degree and he or she was guaranteed employment upon completion of the PhD, it might not be a high priority to choose a very exclusive and probably difficult program since the hurdle of job-hunting is not an issue.[1]

Money

Academia, for many of us "academics," is about some of the best things in life: new ideas, dialogue, problem-solving, etc. However, as much as we would like infinite freedom to sit in a comfortable armchair and read good books, or discuss important ideas with colleagues and peers over coffee, the reality is that we need to have the resources to study and continue to

---

1. Of course, I am not suggesting that one aim high *only* for the sake of attracting the attention of employers. I raise the issue primarily because most doctoral students express concerns about finding a good and suitable position upon completion of their PhD and choose their program with the future and their own employability in mind.

fund our "lives." In the sciences, institutions of higher education tend to have the funding to allow students not to incur too much tuition debt. In the humanities, however, opportunities for salary-like funding for doctoral students are very hard to come by. Therefore, for many prospective doctoral students in biblical studies (and other theological disciplines), it can come down to money. Some doctoral programs, if they offer no help with tuition or with a stipend, can lead students into a debt of over one hundred thousand dollars after the completion of their degree! Other programs, though they might offer a tuition waiver, still leave students with the responsibility for day-to-day expenses. Obviously, if one were wary of accumulating debt from student loans, it would be important to find a "funded" program. However, if money was not an issue—let's say you were awarded some kind of denominational grant or you lived off of personal savings—then you might feel more open to programs that have limited or no funding available. Many of my peers during my doctoral program depended on their spouse's income. Most people survive based on a combination of scholarship aid, earned income, personal savings, loans, and help from friends and relatives.

Time

Doctoral programs in biblical studies vary considerably in terms of length.[2] In the United States, for example, it is often expected that students will complete a PhD in religious studies programs in four to five years. However, the reality is that most students take an additional one to three years to finish. For the completion of a PhD in humanities, the statistic has become rather well known that (1) students can take up to nine to ten years to finish their PhDs, and (2) half of these students don't finish at all.[3] How

2. One should also observe that there is sometimes a discrepancy between the expected length of a program and the actual average length that students take for completion. For example, in the United Kingdom, doctoral programs generally expect a thirty-six-month period of registration, whereas in reality students often require an additional year (and sometimes more) to complete the degree.

3. See the eye-opening study by Ehrenberg et al., "Inside the Black Box," 134–50. Similar findings have been borne out by the study of the Council of Graduate Schools called "The PhD Completion Project" (http://www.phdcompletion.org/); cf. the advice given by The Fund for Theological Education (http://www.fteleaders.org/blog/entry/25-things-you-should-know-before-applying-to-a-ph.d.-program-in-religi). Practically speaking, Yale puts their average rate of completion for department of religion at 6.7 years (http://www.yale.edu/graduateschool/academics/profiles/religiousstudies.

tolerable one considers the amount of time depends significantly on other factors such as financial stability and the level of difficulty of the program (and sometimes the patience of your spouse and children!). Also, it may be important to consider how much coursework you have already undertaken prior to the doctorate. For example, before beginning my doctorate, I had earned a master of divinity (three years) and a master of theology (one year). Therefore, after four years of undergraduate coursework and four years of graduate work, I did not desire to complete another two years of doctoral courses. Alternatively, some students may feel that the additional coursework is necessary for their depth and breadth as a scholar, to help develop a research proposal for the dissertation, and/or to attract the attention of academic employers who often take an interest in those candidates that can teach broadly.

Location

The location of a prospective institution may play an important role in the selection of a doctoral program. Of course, some may prefer to be in sunny southern California, or the culturally and academically attractive environment of Boston. There are other "practical" considerations. Are you restricted to your current area for any reason: specific health needs, proximity to dependents, spouse's workplace, children's school? Does your current financial situation prohibit moving across the country or overseas? Again, one can see that *money*, *time*, and *location* are often interconnected.

Library

Does the research that you desire to do require a specific set of bibliographic resources? I will admit that when I was reviewing various doctoral programs in the United States and the United Kingdom, I glided right over comments about library holdings. Looking back now, it is actually a very important part of the overall experience. Imagine that during both coursework (if applicable) and dissertation writing you need to access two thousand items (articles, books, specialized manuscripts or databases). Consider the amount of time spent locating, collecting, and/or copying these items

pdf); Harvard: six to seven years (http://studyofreligion.fas.harvard.edu/icb/icb.do?keyword=k70796&pageid=icb.page342438); Boston University: seven to eight years (http://www.bu.edu/cas/pdfs/faculty-staff/strategic-data/GRS-HegisStudies-v2.pdf).

if they are not easily available through your institution. Of course, most institutions have some kind of interlibrary loan system, but the delivery time and the cost of late fees may be seriously prohibitive.

Another consideration is whether the topic(s) you wish to pursue require special collections. For instance, some university or seminary libraries will have better references for the study of the Dead Sea scrolls than others. Or, only a select few university libraries may have the kind of resources you may need to study ancient Greek or Roman inscriptions. It is worthwhile to take these very practical sorts of matters into account in the selection of a doctoral program. All things being equal, it is attractive to pursue a school with a larger theology or religious studies collection, but if you are studying such topics like the historical Jesus or justification in Romans, you would probably be safe to assume that most major libraries will have the basic resources.

RANKING INSTITUTIONS: A TIERED APPROACH

It is quite obvious that institutions have their strengths and weaknesses, in terms of academics as well as a number of other qualities. Nevertheless, it is a normal practice and expectation that schools are ranked according to academic excellence. Americans often turn to the *US News and World Report* college and graduate school rankings. In the United Kingdom, several national higher education councils cooperatively sponsor the Research Excellence Framework (REF), which scores and ranks universities according to a number of academic criteria.[4] When it comes to deciding on a graduate school, such general reports can be useful. However, this information tends to be very general, and often one is better advised to focus on the ranking of the particular department of interest. In 2012, R. R. Reno wrote "A 2012 Ranking of Graduate Programs in Theology."[5] Though the list is annotated, it is clearly subjective and certainly looks at the field of theology and religion as a whole. Nevertheless, it is a useful point of entry into the discussion.

For Reno, the ranking is as follows: (1) Duke Divinity School, (2) Notre Dame (Department of Theology), (3) Catholic University, (4) University

4. The REF evaluate scholars based on "the quality of outputs, their impact beyond academia, and the environment that supports research"; see Research Excellence Framework, "What Is the REF?"

5. Reno, "2012 Ranking."

of Toronto, (5) Boston College, (6) Princeton Theological Seminary, (7) Perkins School of Theology (SMU), (8) Yale University, (9) Marquette University, and (10) University of Dayton. Whether or not one agrees with Reno's theological concerns, he goes on to make an important point about selecting the right graduate school: at such a level of study, the quality of the faculty is generally the most important factor. The natural corollary of this fact is that, as professors are constantly moving from one school to another, the ranking will change accordingly.

The approach we will take, instead of merely listing schools (which, again, is subjective and always in flux), is to think in terms of four major categories: first-tier American schools, second-tier American schools, American evangelical seminaries/graduate schools, and British universities. First-tier programs are universities and seminaries that are marked by distinguished faculty, a high level of faculty publishing, strict standards for acceptance, a generous level of student funding available, excellent library holdings and resources, and—usually as a natural outcome of these factors—a high placement for students seeking academic employment (among other things). Second-tier programs, while still excelling in some of these areas, simply do not reach the caliber of the first-tier schools, though in any one or two areas they may be outstanding. Of course, there will inevitably be third-tier and fourth-tier schools (and so forth), but if you are reading this book, chances are you are hoping to find an esteemed program into which you would fit. Therefore, we will only be discussing tier-one and tier-two institutions.

A large number of students choose to study at evangelical seminaries such as Fuller Theological Seminary, Trinity Evangelical Divinity School, Dallas Theological Seminary, and The Southern Baptist Theological Seminary.[6] Offering this group as an entirely separate category does not mean that they are not "first-tier," but, rather, they tend to be discussed and ranked separately as they are mostly private, theologically-oriented institutions (as opposed to divinity schools linked to universities). Some students, especially evangelicals, prefer to study at a theologically-based seminary, so they may prioritize such an institution over other schools. In fact, though, it is often the case that students end up applying to a mixture of schools, some first-tier, some evangelical seminaries, and a few second-tier institutions.

6. The Association of Theological Schools contains over 50 institutional members with doctoral programs.

Below, the factors involved in making such a decision will be discussed further.

A fourth group is British universities. As a graduate of a British university, I often get this question from relatives and friends: "Why did you choose to do your PhD in England?" The fact of the matter is that the study of theological disciplines has a very long and distinguished history in the United Kingdom. Thus, there are a high number of departments of theology and religion that are thriving. Indeed, many of my seminary professors studied in England or Scotland. In fact, in my doctoral program at the University of Durham, the majority of biblical studies doctoral students were American. This is also the case at many major British universities in their theology departments (and especially in biblical studies). In the end, though, the choice of many Americans studying in British universities comes down to the desire to work with particular supervisors on a research project.

FIRST-TIER AMERICAN SCHOOLS VERSUS BRITISH UNIVERSITIES

In general, when graduate students in biblical studies examine the top doctoral programs, attention usually turns to top-tier American schools or prestigious British universities.[7] Before comparing the advantages of each kind of program, we will briefly describe the approach to the doctorate of each type.

First-Tier American Schools

As noted above, schools that typically maintain a first-tier status in the area of New Testament include places like Princeton Theological Seminary, Yale Graduate School, Notre Dame, and Emory Graduate School. Places such as these hold a worldwide reputation of academic excellence. Almost all of these schools are top-notch institutions in a variety of fields and are recognized worldwide for academic excellence. Many of them have historical

7. There are, of course, other possibilities, such as studying in Germany, Australia, or Canada. We will not discuss these programs for two reasons. In the first place, my own experience (in terms of making applications) has been focused on America and the United Kingdom. Secondly, the majority of students of the New Testament study in the latter two places.

connections to a denomination, though for some of these such a history plays only a small role in the current life of the community.

First-tier American programs tend to be five to seven[8] years in length. Almost all American programs require doctoral-level coursework and examinations (typically two to three years) and the writing and defense of a dissertation (typically two to four years). In terms of course and examination structure, students are often required to select a minor field in addition to New Testament. The number of doctoral students in New Testament tends to be quite small, as such places normally accept only a few students in this subdiscipline of religion. As for funding, first-tier American programs tend to be very generous with financial aid packages: usually incoming students receive a tuition waiver or reduction, as well as a living and research stipend. At many of the first-tier schools, additional income can come from teaching fellowships.

British Universities

The British system of education is remarkably different than the American system. In the first place, British PhD programs typically require *no* coursework; the focus of the degree is squarely on the dissertation—both its excellence as a written piece of original research and a successful defense by the student before his or her examiners. Because of the nature of the program (independent research under supervision), the timeframe is normally three years of study. However, in reality, students in biblical studies tend to require more time to complete the degree.

While coursework is not required for the degree and work on the dissertation begins immediately, it is a tradition of most British theology departments to have a New Testament or biblical studies "seminar" that meets regularly. This seminar is not technically a course, but a regularly scheduled meeting for graduate students where a schedule is set up of professional scholars (both from inside the university and outside) who come to the department to "give a paper" (i.e. present a lecture or scholarly proposal).

8. Duke Graduate School lists the average years-to-completion for students in the religion department to be 6.7 years—in the first edition of *Prepare, Succeed, Advance*, about ten years ago, that number was 5.7 years (https://gradschool.duke.edu/about/statistics/all-departments-phd-time-degree-statistics). According to an orientation document for prospective students of Princeton Theological Seminary, the PhD program is designed to be completed in no more than five years of full-time study (see Princeton Theological Seminary, "PhD Studies").

After the paper is presented, there is usually a time of questions, comments, and critical feedback from the audience of students and scholarly staff. Some seminars meet frequently (e.g., once a week), and others meet only occasionally (e.g., twice a semester or term). Students are not usually "required" to attend these seminars, but they are very strongly encouraged to do so to further their breadth of knowledge, develop their understanding of how to develop an argument and utilize evidence, and to engage in the material themselves by offering feedback.

Advantages of the First-Tier American Programs

Funding

It is a serious relief to study in graduate school without incurring too much debt or overextending yourself with earning income outside of the university. Though stipends are not extravagant, many students opt for American first-tier programs largely because of the financial stability that is offered.

Prestige and Excellence

Let's be honest. Many people dream of attending institutions such as Yale and Notre Dame. These schools have reputations for being birthplaces of world-changing ideas, programs, discoveries, and initiatives. As a result, at such places one has the opportunity to learn from world-class faculty, as well as alongside excelling students.

Cross-Discipline Training

As most American first-tier schools have coursework and require a non-New Testament minor, there is a significant element of cross-disciplinary training built into their programs. One can have advanced training in such areas as classics, social sciences, philology and linguistics, and/or ancient Judaism.

Library Holdings

Again, it is easy to underestimate the importance of the quality of the library. To have extensive and often rare book and resource collections means not only that these places are heavily invested in the research of their students, but also that students can progress in their research more quickly and efficiently in comparison to other programs.

Advantages of the British Programs

Prestige and Academic Excellence

Many UK universities, such as Oxford and Cambridge, benefit from world-ranking academic classifications.[9] As such, they certainly rival, in terms of prestige and academic excellence, the American top-tier programs.

International Study

It is usually seen as an advantage to be able to study internationally where one's culturally-formed views are challenged. Also, studying in England offers Americans easy access geographically to places of interest for New Testament research such as Rome, Greece, and Turkey, and also European conferences in places like Germany and Scandinavia. Additionally, if one is interested in the Roman Empire, Britain has much to offer in and of itself, including preserved Roman fortifications, columns, bath houses, and various "Roman Britain" museums and historical records. Finally, the small size of the United Kingdom and the relative ease of travel via train afford an ease of opportunity to travel to other universities for conferences and academic workshops.

---

9. In *US News'* 2018 "World's Best Universities," two British universities (Cambridge and Oxford) rated in the top seven (http:// https://www.usnews.com/education/best-global-universities/).

Program Length

If one has studied in higher education for five to six years, entering a lengthy doctoral program could be daunting. The British programs, as they are solely focused on the dissertation, allow students to finish in about three years.

No Coursework

Closely related to the program length is the fact that there is no coursework in traditional British programs. For those who desire coursework at the doctoral level, obviously this is not an advantage. However, for many students, having no coursework or examinations (other than the dissertation defense) allows a significant measure of freedom to publish articles and attend conferences.

SECOND-TIER AMERICAN SCHOOLS

Our classification of "second-tier" American schools refers to those institutions that offer graduate programs in biblical studies, but are not of the same caliber as the widely recognized first-tier schools. It should be recognized that one can have an excellent education at such a place; perhaps even better than at some of the first-tier schools. The fact of the matter is, though, that institutions are often compared according to broad criteria and based on reputation, prestige, and history, these schools are not as exclusive or academically-recognized. The program structure at these institutions is very similar to the first-tier programs: five to seven years in length, with a system composed of coursework, examinations, and dissertation research.

Advantages of the Second-Tier American Programs

Potential for Acceptance

A second-tier program, as it is by definition lower in rank than the first-tier programs, would attract fewer students. Thus, the likelihood of being accepted would increase.

World-Class Faculty

Despite the fact that such places are not Ivy League institutions, often the biblical studies faculty members at these schools are still considered to be experts in their various fields, and the overall education can be very rewarding.

Disadvantages of the Second-Tier American Programs

Funding

It is typical that second-tier programs rarely offer full-funding (let alone living stipends) to more than a select group of people. Thus, one must face the prospect that the five to seven years will involve major financial debt. Some schools can provide teaching fellowships and other "working" scholarships, but again, these tend to be few in number and they often fall below the rate of remuneration found at first-tier schools.

Employment Potential

Again, there are many factors that play into how one gets a job, but it is a reality of the discipline of biblical studies in general that first-tier schools are perceived as more rigorous, exclusive, and of a higher caliber in education. Thus, the first-tier students have a higher potential, from an institutional standpoint, of employability.

AMERICAN EVANGELICAL SEMINARIES

As mentioned above, there are dozens of well-respected evangelical seminaries that offer doctorates in biblical studies. The program structure, again, is similar to other American institutions in terms of length (five to seven years) and structure (coursework, examinations, and dissertation).

Advantages of American Evangelical Seminary Programs

Potential for Acceptance

While usually maintaining a high standard, seminaries tend to have the resources and desire to accept a higher number of students than first-tier schools. The obvious result is that one's chances of getting a place in a program are more predictable.

Potential for Faith-Based Learning

Some students find it a distinct advantage, or perhaps even crucial, to study in a faith-based environment where certain doctrinal or theological distinctives are upheld (such as the authority of Scripture).

Denominational Affiliation

Those schools that are denominationally affiliated can be attractive if the student comes from that tradition and has a desire to seek academic employment in the same denomination. Some hiring institutions, in fact, *expect* prospective professors to have their doctoral degree from a school of their own denomination. Such practical considerations can have a major impact on the choice of a doctoral program.

Disadvantages of American Evangelical Seminaries

Funding

Much like the second-tier programs, the evangelical seminaries tend to offer less funding than the first-tier, or if full funding (with a living stipend) is available, it is only for a very select few.

Potential Limitation of Employment

The faith-based nature of seminaries has a double effect, it would seem, for employment. On the one hand, if you are seeking employment primarily in Christian universities and seminaries, it is can be seen as valuable to study in a confessional program. However, the opposite effect could happen as well. If you are seeking employment at secular or public institutions (or those that do not value conservative viewpoints or faith-based learning), your application may be discounted on these grounds. Again, the reality is that most students tend to apply to whatever jobs are being advertised, as the number of positions are limited, and this involves a mixture of Christian and non-Christian institutions. Overall, from my own experience, Christian institutions respect degrees from non-Christian and Christian programs, while there is a strong tendency for non-Christians schools to treat doctoral degrees from seminaries with suspicion (both academically and doctrinally).[10]

RANKING THE PROGRAMS

I hesitate to offer a listing of the various tiered programs, because it will inevitably be subjective based on my own knowledge of the field and my experience. Moreover, it should be recognized that ratings are based, to a significant degree, on the faculty present at any given institution, and the list could change drastically in a matter of a few years. Nevertheless, for those readers that desire even a basic list, just to get an idea of where to start researching and looking, I humbly offer a list of schools that currently fit this category:

First-Tier American Programs (in Alphabetical Order)

- Baylor University
- Duke Graduate School
- Emory University

10. Some of this, perhaps, comes from ignorance about what goes on in a seminary program. Those who have never studied in such an environment might guess or presume that these programs are not rigorous or "critical" in terms of method and approach. In my experience, there are some seminaries that rival the first-tier schools in terms of difficulty, advancement of research, and exploration of new methodologies.

- Harvard Graduate School
- Marquette University
- Princeton Theological Seminary
- University of Notre Dame
- Yale University

British Universities (in Alphabetical Order)

- University of Aberdeen
- University of Cambridge
- University of Durham
- University of Edinburgh
- University of Manchester
- University of Oxford
- University of St. Andrews

American Evangelical Seminaries (and Graduate Schools)

- Asbury Theological Seminary
- Dallas Theological Seminary
- Fuller Theological Seminary
- The Southern Baptist Theological Seminary
- Trinity Evangelical Divinity School
- Westminster Theological Seminary
- Wheaton Graduate School

Let me reiterate, again, that this list is not meant to be exhaustive, nor does it reflect a ranking of schools from best to worst. It is merely a sample of schools that fit these kinds of categories. It is up to each individual and their priorities and desires to decide what a hierarchy of "best schools" would look like. This decision, again, would be based on your timeframe, financial situation, academic achievements, theological interests, ability to relocate, vocational goals, and also potentially philosophical, religious, and denominational considerations.[11] And, again, the lists of high-ranking schools will change from year to year, largely based on the movement and/ or retirement of attractive faculty members.

Looking broadly at the kinds of doctoral programs is a necessary prerequisite to the work of actually preparing for entrance into one. In the next chapter, we will venture into the details of what admissions committees are looking for and on what basis they choose their best candidates. Before that, I want to briefly address online/distance PhD programs.

ONLINE AND DISTANCE PHD PROGRAMS IN BIBLICAL STUDIES

One of the most frequent questions that I am asked via Facebook, email, or in person is whether there are legitimate distance-learning options for the PhD. The reality is, there are many intellectually capable and eager students who simply cannot move to take up residency for several years in a traditional learning environment. Perhaps they have dependents to take care of in a fixed location. Maybe a spouse is working and they must stay put. And now, well into the twenty-first century, good technology exists to make distance learning vibrant and engaging. So, many are wondering if they can stay where they are and get a good PhD.

The answer to that question twenty years ago was no. The answer now is probably not. Yes, there are several American schools that now offer an online PhD program in theology, biblical studies, church history, etc. But no elite schools offer such an option. UK universities appear to be opening up distance-learning possibilities; most religion and theology departments continue the British tradition of the PhD, focusing on independent research and not coursework, so practically speaking it makes sense that meeting "online" with a supervisor would suffice. But even if some UK departments make this opportunity possible, it continues to be viewed as

11. My own journey was as follows. I had an interest in studying in an ecumenical and rigorously academic environment with a world-class faculty and a reputation for excellence. I was interested in a place where traditional exegetical methods were employed, but there was some interest in theology and sociology. While I did not desire to study at an evangelical institution *per se*, I hoped to find a place where I would not be hastily labeled and looked down upon because of my confessional interests. I pursued the following schools: Yale, Princeton, Emory, Notre Dame, University of Oxford (England), University of Durham (England), University of St. Andrews (Scotland), and University of Aberdeen (Scotland).

a lesser experience. There is no comprehensive list of institutions offering distance/online options for the PhD. Just by a quick Google search, I found several UK programs that explicitly mention distance options (e.g., Birmingham, Aberdeen, and Edinburgh).[12] Other schools allow distance living, but require the student to come to campus one or twice a year for face-to-face supervision.[13]

My general approach to thinking about distance-learning PhD programs is this: there are several major downsides to this way of earning a PhD, and therefore it is not ideal and even discouraged; however, if the PhD cannot be done in residency, there are some good options. But *why* is it discouraged? There is the stigma that this is a lazy form of education for the student, as if it is a hobby or a matter of convenience. Whether or not this perception is accurate, it persists nevertheless. More importantly, while it is true that digital educational technology has improved, there is still something special about regular, in-person communal learning that you can't replicate online. Also, the reality is that networking plays such a crucial role in getting a job and navigating AAR/SBL, and distance students tend to be isolated.

When students ask me about distance PhD programs, I tend to discourage this option. The best path to getting a good education and then getting a job in the academy is to "go big"; aim to enter into a top-tier PhD program, and fully immerse yourself in the academic world. There are certainly stories of people doing distance programs and then finding gainful employment in teaching. But these are few, and such exceptions probably involve *exceptional* people that also found a bit of luck.

Now, if it comes down to it, and you simply *can't* move to a top-tier institution, and your only options *are* distance programs, I think there are some ways to "close the gap," as it were. First, you will need to foster some kind of learning community. It may be through your doctoral institution—perhaps they have a weekly seminar that you can engage via Skype or Zoom. It is best if it is more than a one-off; it ought to be regular. Go to academic conferences, intentionally meet peers, and give presentations. And, if you can, publish an article or two with a major journal. Some students

12. https://www.birmingham.ac.uk/postgraduate/courses/research/thr/theology-and-religion.aspx; https://www.abdn.ac.uk/sdhp/courses/research-by-distance-learning-1352.php; https://www.ed.ac.uk/studying/postgraduate/degrees/index.php?r=site/bySubject&sid=36.

13. Durham University explicitly mentions this expectation: https://www.dur.ac.uk/theology.religion/postgrad/researchdegrees/residence/.

overcompensate by self-publishing or publishing with several low-tier journals—don't do this. Quality over quantity is crucial.

2

Preparing for Doctoral Studies
From Education to Application

It is not the experience of many people that they graduate from their master's program and then "decide" to do a PhD. In most cases, a lot of preparation work comes before the application. It often takes years to make headway in biblical studies and build up an impressive resume that will aid in securing a place in a coveted program. The goal is not to meet the minimum expectations as an applicant, but to far exceed expectations. When admissions committees have to sort through many dozens of applications, you want your cover letter and dossier to be impossible to ignore. In the following pages, we will discuss what it will take to accomplish that.

EIGHT FACTORS

When you consider the criteria on the basis of which committees sort through and select applicants, there appear to be eight primary factors: institutions of education, grade point average, preparatory coursework, references, standardized test scores, research/publishing record, teaching experience, and institutional "fit." Not all of these factors will apply in all circumstances. For example, most British universities do not require American students to submit Graduate Record Examination scores.[1] Also,

---

1. Cambridge University is the only British university I am aware of that *does* require American students to submit GRE scores.

the weight given to each area is not equal, and the balances differ from one place to the next. Nevertheless, thinking ahead about these factors should provide the appropriate amount of preparation for students with a view towards most programs. Interactions with recent graduates of an institution of interest may offer insight into how that school weighs these factors.

Institutions of Education

Where you studied prior to applying for a doctoral program is obviously an important indicator of suitability for admissions committees. However, they are not necessarily always looking for students who studied at Ivy League schools. Rather, you will want to make sure you choose places to study that have a solid reputation for respected faculty and an overall pursuit and achievement of excellence.

As we are dealing with religious studies, it is inevitable that some programs and schools may be biased against other schools showing distaste for certain doctrinal affirmations, approaches, or styles. While you do not need to compromise your own beliefs, showing an awareness and appreciation for a variety of perspectives and approaches may pacify some of these concerns. In my own experience, though, many doctoral programs encourage diversity of thought, background, and tradition.

Grade Point Average

The American educational system, whether we like it or not, depends on the grade point average (GPA) for assessing and comparing academic performance. From elementary school through to the highest levels of study, you are scored on a scale from 0.0 to 4.0. It is no surprise, then, to learn that doctoral programs in biblical studies look closely at the student's GPA.

Of course first-tier programs have exceptionally high standards when it comes to the GPA. Most admissions reports will state that there is no magic number to achieve, and that is true. They do not want to deter anyone from applying just because they don't meet a stated standard—they recognize that some exceptional students may fall a bit below. Nevertheless, it is helpful to have some indication of what is average or expected. There appears to be a general standard of working upward from the A- range, which begins at 3.4. In reality, though, the average of *accepted* students is probably somewhere closer to 3.8.[2] Again, that does not mean that rejection is certain below this, or that acceptance is certain above this. Rather, it is useful to know where you stand with regard to *general* expectations. One indicator of achievement is the cutoff marks for graduating with distinction. At my undergraduate institution, a 3.5 or better was needed to graduate *cum laude*, a 3.75 or better for *magna cum laude*, and 3.9 or better for *summa cum laude*. American evangelical seminaries also maintain high academic standards for the GPA, though because many such programs can accept several students, the competition is not as fierce.[3] Overall, it is advisable to aim for a GPA higher than a 3.5, though, again, in reality accepted students would have probably exceeded these expectations on average.

The situation is a bit different when applying to study in the United Kingdom. Due to the high number of Americans that study at the PhD level in biblical studies there, admissions committees are undoubtedly familiar with the GPA system. However, they tend to be less discriminating when it comes to looking for a particular number.

As will be discussed further under "preparatory coursework" and "institutions of education," it is not enough to have a high GPA. It matters, with regard to GPA, what kinds of courses were taken and where. Generally speaking, the GPA of your master's work from higher institutions matters most, as well as the courses/majors that relate most closely to the area of study for which you are applying (i.e., Old Testament/New Testament). This means that if you struggled in your undergraduate program, a lower GPA may not signal rejection as long as the master's work is sufficiently impressive. On the other hand, it may not mean as much to an admissions committee if you earned a 4.0 in your undergraduate if the major was in a completely unrelated field.

Preparatory Coursework

Beyond a glance at the GPA, admissions committees are interested in the kind of coursework a prospective student has done. One of the reasons why transcripts are required is because they want to inspect the breadth and

2. See, for example, Duke Graduate School's statistics: http://gradschool.duke.edu/about/statistics/admitrel.htm.

3. Duke Graduate School has about ten students graduating per year (http://www.duke.edu/web/gradreligion/documents/NRCAssessment.pdf), while many evangelical seminaries will have thirty to fifty students graduating.

depth of the courses taken and how prepared the student is for doctoral-level courses and/or professional research. Especially for biblical studies, six dimensions of an education round out the preparatory coursework: biblical content, hermeneutics, backgrounds, languages, history of interpretation, and critical thinking skills.

In terms of *biblical content*, there is obviously going to be the expectation that the prospective student is actually acquainted with the biblical texts, both generally and specifically in the area of interest. This usually comes through survey and exegesis courses. It should not take a book like this to tell you that such preparation is essential. The more common problem is that seminary students (in particular) assume that exegesis courses are most important and focus on them to the neglect of the other preparatory ones. As with all things, balance is crucial.

An advanced understanding of *hermeneutics*, the study of the principles of interpretation, is absolutely essential to good preparation in biblical studies. Normally a graduate degree in biblical studies will require a basic hermeneutics course, but it is advisable to learn about more advanced methods in use in your field(s) of interest. While your master's institution may offer such a course, it may happen that you will need to design an independent study course that will meet these needs.[4] It may be profitable to choose one advanced exegetical tool to study for an independent course such as social-scientific criticism, rhetorical criticism, or narrative criticism.

It is also difficult to overestimate the utility of studying biblical *backgrounds*. For Old Testament study, this would largely involve Ancient Near Eastern backgrounds, and for the New Testament, Jewish and Greco-Roman ones. Much advanced research at the doctoral level involves an awareness of and interactions with texts, artifacts, and developments that arise from these ancient worlds and how they inform, overlap with, support, and challenge voices in the Bible. Later I will adumbrate what is basically expected of a New Testament doctoral student with respect to such knowledge.

In terms of early Judaism, one should have a grasp of several features: (1) the general history of the Jewish people in the second temple period; (2) the most insightful and significant works produced during this time (e.g., the Dead Sea Scrolls, the works of Philo and Josephus, the LXX [including

---

4. Some important resources to consider in this area would be John Barton's *The Cambridge Companion to Biblical Interpretation*, Paula Gooder's *Searching for Meaning*, and Joel B. Green's *Hearing the New Testament*.

the Old Testament Apocrypha], the Old Testament Pseudepigrapha, etc.); (3) the culture and social dynamics of that period; and (4) the methods of interpretation common at the time (*pesher, midrash,* etc.). A helpful place to begin such a study is with George W. E. Nickelsburg's *Jewish Literature between the Bible and the Mishnah.* A wellspring of information can also be found in Craig A. Evans and Stanley E. Porter's *Dictionary of New Testament Background* (*DNTB*).

Equally important for New Testament study is a grasp of the Greco-Roman world in which the early church was born. Again, it is important to know: (1) the general history of the classical world, hellenization, and the rise of the Roman Empire; (2) the literature of the Greeks and Romans (broadly); (3) the religions and religious atmosphere of the Greco-Roman world (including the imperial cult); (4) Greco-Roman rhetoric (again, broadly); (5) the secular ethics and popular philosophies of the times; and (6) the basic geography of the Roman Empire, with specific attention to major cities in Asia Minor, Macedonia, and Italia. Alongside consulting the *DNTB*, students are often directed to James Jeffers's *The Greco-Roman World of the New Testament Era.* Also very useful are Warren Carter's *The Roman Empire and the New Testament: An Essential Guide* and Paul Sampley's edited volume *Paul in the Greco-Roman World.*

In terms of the general study of backgrounds of the New Testament, two more suggestions can be made. One should be aware of the eminent book series called *Aufstieg und Niedergang der römischen Welt* (in English, *Rise and Fall of the Roman World*), which treats numerous aspects of the ancient Roman world, including politics, literature, philosophy, arts, and religion. The many contributors come from various fields, including classics and religious studies. Some of the articles are written by biblical scholars.[5] Secondly, there are a number of textbooks in existence that offer readings of primary texts such as C. K. Barrett's *New Testament Background: Selected Documents.* Another option is *Readings from the First-Century World: Primary Sources for New Testament Study,* edited by Walter A. Elwell and Robert W. Yarbrough, which has an Old Testament counterpart: *Readings from the Ancient Near East: Primary Sources for Old Testament Study,* edited by Bill T. Arnold and Brian Beyer. In the end, it may be most profitable to create your own list of texts by mixing and matching, alongside following the recommendations of your academic course advisor.

5. A searchable database of the article titles can be found at http://www.cs.uky.edu/~raphael/scaife/anrw.html.

Another option for gaining some of this experience with background material is to see if your current institution is part of a local consortium. This could open up the door to courses not available at your school and it may lead to developing a relationship with another professor that could one day serve as a referee.[6]

Studying backgrounds is not just another hoop that one must jump through, but is absolutely essential for a precise understanding of what is going on in the biblical texts. In fact, it is often the case that acquaintance with parallel ancient texts inspires theories and ideas that become doctoral project proposals. Thus, it is important to read these texts actively, thinking through convergences and divergences with the ideas and theological perspectives of the biblical authors.

A large part of doctoral research is interaction with the biblical texts in their original *languages*. In seminary or graduate school, it is common to study Greek and/or Hebrew at the basic level. For doctoral studies, though, the expectations in terms of language skill are very high. For New Testament, it goes without saying that the candidate knows Koine Greek very well (in terms of grammar, syntax, and vocabulary). In general, it would be advisable to know the New Testament Greek vocabulary down to words that occur twenty times or less. An advanced knowledge of grammar can be gained through studying Daniel B. Wallace's *Greek Grammar Beyond the Basics*, or the more recent offering by David Mathewson and Elodie Ballantine Emig, *Intermediate Greek Grammar*. New Testament exegesis classes will further strengthen one's knowledge of New Testament Greek. After getting a sufficient amount of grammar under one's belt, the most profitable thing to do is *read, read, read*! That is, take rapid reading courses where you just read through a large number of texts without taking too much time to analyze it theologically or rhetorically. I regularly recommend to students, as a must-have resource, *The UBS Greek New Testament: A Reader's Edition*, which offers a "contextualized translation at the bottom of the page of all vocabulary items occurring thirty times or fewer in the New Testament." Additionally, a dictionary is appended to the back that has lexical entries for the remaining words that occur thirty times or more.

Aside from studying New Testament Greek, you can further strengthen your language skills by exposure to Attic Greek, the most important and influential dialect of classical antiquity.[7] Many students of the New Testa-

6. A "referee" is a term used to designate someone that writes references.

7. One might consult the Joint Association of Classical Teachers' *A Greek Anthology*

ment also find it helpful to engage with the style, grammar, and vocabulary of the Septuagint.[8] Finally, one might consider studying the Greek of the church fathers.[9] Conceivably, a course could be designed that worked through a sampling from various materials and periods.[10]

For students of the New Testament, it is also important to know the original language(s) of the Old Testament. Hebrew is, of course, often required in master of divinity programs. For academic study, it is invaluable. For instance, when looking at the New Testament quotations and allusions of the Old Testament, it is helpful to note the differences between the LXX text and the Hebrew Masoretic text to discern whether the New Testament writer was relying on one of these as the *vorlage* (the underlying text). Beyond a basic first year of grammar, an intermediate course in Hebrew grammar and a set of readings can really enhance your understanding of the Old Testament language and literature.[11]

There are a number of other ancient languages that one could learn with profit. Aramaic, for example, is a Semitic language that could be useful if one were studying portions of Old Testament, such as the Aramaic parts of Daniel and Ezra. It is also useful for studying the Second Temple *targumim* or the Elephantine papyri. Syriac is a particular dialect of Aramaic, and learning this language affords one access to the Peshitta.

Another important ancient language is Latin. At the most utilitarian level, many scholarly terms and abbreviations are in Latin. In addition, classical Latin offers the ability to read Roman literature that can inform our reading of the New Testament. Ecclesiastical Latin can aid in reading early church liturgies, epistles, and early commentaries. Latin can also be very handy for purposes of textual criticism—regarding especially the Old Latin manuscripts as well as the Vulgate.[12]

---

for a list of readings.

8. A number of reading texts can be found in Rodney J. Decker's *Koine Greek Reader*.

9. Again, consult Decker's *Koine Greek Reader* and its relevant sections; also Rodney A. Whitacre's *Patristic Greek Reader*; cf. Michael W. Holmes, *Apostolic Fathers*.

10. In 2018, I coedited a graded reader called *Intermediate Biblical Greek Reader: Galatians and Related Texts*. This textbook offers guided readings from Galatians, James, the Septuagint, and a reading from St. John Chrysostom. It is an "open textbook," which means it is freely available online. See the bibliography for more details.

11. One example of a reader text would be Donald R. Vance's *Hebrew Reader for Ruth*; for more advanced study, see Ben Zvi et al., *Readings in Biblical Hebrew*.

12. For a reliable introductory textbook for classical Latin, one can hardly do better than *Wheelock's Latin*; for the Latin of the early church, see Collins, *Primer of Ecclesiastical*

There is a common expectation that well-prepared doctoral students can not only engage well with the biblical text, but also the relevant secondary literature. While many books, essays, and articles are in English, there is also a wealth of information relevant to biblical studies in German and French. It is highly recommended that a basic knowledge of German grammar is acquired before beginning a doctoral program. Acquiring this language knowledge can happen in a number of ways. One route is to take a course (or series of courses). It is not necessarily the best option to take a traditional modern German language course. These kinds of courses tend to focus on carrying on everyday conversations, are often pitched at students that have never learned a language before, and frequently work at such a slow pace that one must advance through three to four levels to progress to reasonable fluency. What a doctoral student in biblical studies needs is competency in *reading*, not necessarily *speaking*. More suitable would be a course specifically designed for graduate students who are learning a language only for reading academic works. These sorts of classes are not uncommon. For example, Harvard offers a summer course called "Introduction to German for Reading Knowledge." A course like this introduces the student to basic grammar and requires her to learn vocabulary that is most important for academic study.

Another option, if you are not able to enroll in a grammar course, is to develop an independent study course. There are two excellent textbooks specifically geared towards teaching basic grammar to graduate students for research purposes: April Wilson's *German Quickly: A Grammar for Reading German*, and Richard Alan Korb's *Jannach's German for Reading Knowledge*. I tend to refer students to Wilson's textbook, as she includes some theological and philosophical reading exercises.[13] Aside from learning foundational grammar, the most profitable route for strengthening German knowledge is simply to read German. I highly recommend *Modern Theological German: A Reader and Dictionary*, which works through a number of biblical texts in German and progresses to excerpts from theologians such as Martin Luther, Adolf Schlatter, and Karl Barth, giving grammatical helps along the way. Again, once basic grammatical concepts and paradigms are committed to memory, one is best served by a trial-and-error approach

---

Latin.

13. More bibliographic and research advice pertaining to German study and usage appears in the discussion of dissertation writing in [x-ref].

where you attempt to translate a text and then compare your work with a professional translation.

Is it acceptable to learn German "on my own," without a course? From one perspective, the only thing that really matters is that you know enough German to work well with the secondary literature of your field. However, two factors are important to consider. First, it takes a lot of self-motivation and discipline to sustain a regular program of language study. For most people, it is important, and sometimes necessary, to have the built-in work of regular tutorials, graded assignment, and the ability to ask questions and interact with others. Also, having peers who are going through the same language battle can be an important source of encouragement and motivation. Secondly, it is difficult to prove your level of proficiency on doctoral applications without evidence from your transcripts.

How do you know when you have learned enough German? My recommendation is that you should be able to translate a scholarly piece of work at the rate of one page every 15–20 minutes with the aid of your grammar helps and a German-English dictionary. It is not unreasonable to aim for this goal with two graduate-level independent study courses that work through a basic textbook such as Wilson or Kolb/Jannach.

Though German is, by far, the most important modern language that students of the Bible need to learn (aside from English), there is also a good amount of literature in French. Once you have built up a comfortable proficiency in German, a course of study in French is highly recommended. For many doctoral programs, some training in German is assumed (prior to application) and French is "highly recommended." Obviously, to put oneself in the most impressive position, facility with both is encouraged. In terms of resources, I have found no better textbook than K. C. Sandberg and Eddison C. Tatham's *French for Reading*, which follows a similar teaching philosophy as the German books mentioned above.

One final recommendation: while the goal is to be able to read German and French, and it is not necessary to learn to speak fluently, many students I know have benefited greatly from spending some time learning these languages (or practicing them) in Germany and/or France. The Goethe-Institut offers a very flexible program of language study in Germany that provides world-class grammatical instruction alongside immersion in the culture.[14]

---

14. Visit their website at www.goethe.de/enindex.htm.

To summarize this section on language learning, for those studying New Testament, my recommendations for proficiency are as follows: Greek (high), Hebrew (moderate), German (moderate), French (basic), Latin (basic), Aramaic (basic). Ideally, prior to applying for a doctoral program, a student will have secured knowledge of Greek, Hebrew, and some German.[15]

References

A standard part of doctoral applications is scholarly references. Academic references give a personal look into the lives of the applicants and serve as further evidence that the prospective student is the kind of person represented in the transcripts and curricula vitae (CV). Typically, an application will require between two to four recommendations from professors that you have known for at least a year (but preferably two or more). It is important to choose your referees carefully. You want to maintain a good balance between picking someone that adores you and will say the "right things" and someone who is well-known but cannot speak knowledgably about your coursework and research capabilities. Here are a few principles to help guide how you shape and build relationships.

First, aim for at least one "senior scholar" referee. A senior scholar is someone who has gained a high level of respect in his or her field (usually through publishing, teaching, and discipline leadership). Normally, to obtain a good recommendation from such a person, you would need to take a course (ideally two or more) from him or her and do well enough to draw attention. This should not be done as a sycophant, but by hard work and a genuine interest in the course content.

If you can obtain references from three senior scholars, that is admirable and will strengthen an application. However, it is difficult to have close contact with so many of them and, thus, it is inevitable for most people that recommendations come from other educators. It is important to ensure that all referees are men and women of integrity and that they know the applicant well enough to give an informed reflection on his or her suitability for doctoral work.

It is helpful to aim for some diversity in your referees. Your application can appear a bit bland if all three references come from New Testament (or

15. For Old Testament study: Hebrew (high), Greek (moderate), Aramaic (moderate), Akkadian (moderate), Ugaritic (moderate), Latin (basic).

Old Testament) scholars from the same situation. A better scenario would be to have at least one reference from another institution (e.g., if you studied at one place for a master of divinity, and at another place for a master of theology).

Thirdly, help your referee by preparing a set of informative personal materials. Though referees may like you and show eagerness to endorse your application, they are often writing recommendations for numerous people, and sometimes forget specific achievements. A list of items to help them write their recommendations may include transcripts (undergraduate and graduate), your CV, and a writing sample. You may also want to include, for the referee, personal information about nonacademic achievements, ministry involvement (if applicable and relevant), and significant cross-cultural experiences. Imagine yourself in the position of the one writing the reference—what kind of information would you want and need to know to write an accurate and appealing endorsement?

You may also want to furnish your referees with your research proposal if the program to which you are applying requires one (e.g., British programs and American ones such as Wheaton Graduate School). This allows the referee to make useful connections between your topic of interest and those courses which you took that contributed to your knowledge of that area.

How can I know if a referee will write something good? It is helpful to keep in mind that the referee usually knows that the student is specifically relying on good references to gain admission into a doctoral program. Nevertheless, we have all heard horror stories about negative references. To be clear, it is poor practice to open a reference without the permission of the referee. In many cases, the referee will be required (by the doctoral program standards) to seal the envelope, place a piece of tape over the flap, and sign across it to prove that the student has not looked at it. A helpful way to know for sure how the referee feels about your work is to ask him or her in person. Set up a time to sit down with a potential referee and say, "I am interested in applying for a doctoral program at [such and such a university]. Do you think I am ready for that academic level? Would you be willing to write a *strong* reference for me?" It would be unusual for the professor to give you direct feedback that would contradict what he or she would write on paper.

Standardized Test Scores (Julianna Smith)[16]

The GRE (Graduate Record Exam) is a standard admissions requirement for many graduate programs. There are two different types of exams: subject tests and the general test. Many graduate programs only require the general test, although it is a good idea to look at your desired program's requirement before beginning the exam preparation process.

The general test (the most commonly required test for biblical studies, religion, etc. programs) is a 225-minute, computer-based test divided into three sections. The first section is analytical writing, and it tests critical thinking, the ability to develop coherent ideas on complex issues and clarity of written expression. The writing section contains two writing prompts: analyze an issue and analyze an argument. Test-takers are given thirty minutes for each prompt.

The second section is the verbal reasoning section. It evaluates the test-taker's ability to discern relationships between words and clauses, as well as analyze written material. One of the challenging parts of this section is its breadth of vocabulary. It requires the examinee to use words she might not use in daily discourse. The written material presented for analysis may cover a variety of subjects, including literature, history, "hard sciences," and social sciences, etc. This section is divided into two thirty-minute units.

The final section is the quantitative reasoning. This section covers basic problem-solving and evaluation of quantitative data and requires the use of arithmetic, basic algebra and geometry, and data analysis. This section does not measure the test-taker's ability to use advanced mathematical concepts. The quantitative analysis section is divided into two thirty-five-minute units.

During the exam, time is allotted for a short break. Some test-takers may receive additional test sections for research purposes, which are unscored. As the test-taker, you may or may not be informed if you are receiving an unscored section; therefore, it is in your interest to treat each section as if it will be included in your final score.

There are a blessed few people applying for graduate programs who will clear the GRE hurdle with grace and ease. Many more will struggle through this test, and their scores will be more reflective of their grit and tenacity than verbal or quantitative ability. Accept early in the process that

---

16. This section on the GRE was kindly written by Julianna Smith, a former student of mine at Portland Seminary and currently a doctoral student at UCLA.

preparing for the test might take more hours than you want to give it and more money than you want to spend on it.

One of the important keys to scoring well on this exam is familiarity with the types of questions the GRE asks. Through repeated exposure, one learns the logic of the test. This is important because most people do not encounter test questions like those on the GRE anywhere in their university education. Related to this is training to sit for a 225-minute exam. Even if one has mastered the material covered in the test, he might not have ever had to maintain that level of focus for that long. Learning the test form matters almost as much as mastering the test content.

How can one appropriately prepare for this form of exam? Taking a series of full-length, scored practice tests is the best way. There are many GRE test-preparation companies that sell this type of practice test. While investing in these scored practice tests might not be the way anyone wants to spend their money, most of the tests will analyze the test-taker's performance and identify content areas in need of improvement. Equipped with these analytics, it is easier to determine which content areas to study. After studying those content areas, one should take another test and see if the score has improved to an acceptable level, repeating the process as necessary. These practice tests, running about twenty US dollars apiece, can give one a good sense for how she might perform. This investment pays off in the long run. It is much cheaper to buy multiple practice tests than to pay to take the actual test, running around two hundred US dollars, more than once.

Each graduate committee functions differently and gives each of the component parts of the application different weight. It is probably safe to say that most programs are not heavily weighting the applicant's GRE score when they consider all of the application materials. That said, a poor score does not ever do the applicant any favors. Elite programs attract elite candidates, and it is accurate to assume these programs will annually attract multiple applicants who have flawless transcripts, strong recommendations, and compelling writing samples. In this type of applicant pool, a good GRE score demonstrates a certain consistency in academic performance, and a poor score may eliminate an application from consideration.

In order to determine the score for which you should aim, check the website of the department/college to which you are applying. Sometimes you can find information on the average GRE scores of admitted applicants or "tips" for applying. Most schools do not publish a minimally acceptable

GRE score, so determining a score for which to aim is highly subjective. By way of anecdote, committees for biblical studies, history, and the like are more concerned about verbal and writing scores than quantitative analysis scores. Again, however, in a strong applicant pool, there is less room for application weaknesses—even a quantitative analysis score. Although identifying a definitive score for which to aim is fraught with challenges, elite programs in biblical studies *generally* accept applicants with verbal scores of 160 or higher, quantitative scores of 151 or higher, and analytical writing scores of five or higher.

Research/Publishing Record

Beyond taking certain courses and acquiring various degrees, a good doctoral program will be impressed to see any published work or evidence of scholarly interaction. At the undergraduate and master's level, it is rare to see students who have published books and articles (though not impossible!). There are a number of ways to get experience in this area. One route is to try and publish a book review.[17] Another option is to become a part-time research assistant for a professor of your current institution and ask him or her if you can contribute, even if in a small way, to their work. Perhaps it may only be by working on an index or bibliography, but any experience is useful. A third consideration is presenting an academic paper at a conference.[18] Finally, there may be some merits to beginning an academic blog. Any practice that you can get writing, revising, and thinking on paper (or screen!) contributes to improving the process of reflection and communication. It has yet to be seen, though, how blogs are viewed in terms of academic validity. Merely writing for a blog will not instantly give credibility; content is certainly the key to proving the worth of one's writing and research skills.

Teaching Experience

Teaching is, of course, the ultimate goal of many students who wish to pursue a doctorate. However, very few students have the opportunity to teach

17. A more thorough discussion of how to write and publish a book review appears in [x-ref].

18. A more thorough discussion of how to write an academic paper and get it accepted appears in [x-ref].

prior to beginning a postgraduate program. Seminaries in particular rarely have teaching fellowships available to master's students. But, if your institution does have teaching assistants for biblical studies, Greek, or Hebrew, it is a worthwhile opportunity. Aside from the assumption that it looks good on a CV, it allows you to sample the atmosphere of the lecturer/instructor and see if it is a good vocational match. It also provides a context for creativity, a place to learn pedagogical skills, and an atmosphere where you must learn to be clear, direct, and organized.

Other possibilities to pursue are teaching as an adjunct instructor at a local community college or working with any schools that have online teaching opportunities. And, of course, there may be occasions in faith-community settings for teaching non-academics. Any little bit can help to gain experience and also to demonstrate skills in communication and pedagogy.

Institutional "Fit"

Prospective doctoral students are often wise to send out a set of applications to several programs—elite programs have very limited spots, so the theory is that *applying to more programs increases the chances of acceptance somewhere.* Indeed, applying to more than one program is advised. But the danger in applying to several programs is the temptation to reuse application materials like CV, cover letter, application essays, etc. This can give such materials a generic quality. But it is important to know that admissions committees are eager to know (a) the student has a specific interest in *their* program with its distinctives and (b) the application materials demonstrate that the prospective student will contribute meaningfully to that particular programs research interests. Thus, while reuse of some application materials is necessary and unproblematic, each application to each program ought to address that program's unique faculty and program interests.

The "X" Factor

We have addressed eight elements that appear to factor into doctoral admissions. But there is another dimension that we can add that should not be ignored—what I call the "X" factor. In the end, one can check every box, so to speak, and follow every recommendation and still not find a place in a good program. The simple reason is *competition*—admissions committees have to sort through (sometimes) over a hundred applicants, which include dozens of highly qualified candidates. The only way to get noticed is to be *noticeable*. There is no magic formula for how to do that. The first step is awareness that most of the applicants have good grades, good references, and studied at good schools. You have to ask yourself, *what can I offer that is unique?* One way to distinguish yourself is to "diversify" your background and portfolio.

Diversification can occur on many levels. One is, of course, the institution(s) of education. Studying for one bachelor's degree and two master's degrees at the same institution can give the impression that a student has had a very homogenous and one-dimensional education. Compare that with a student that went to a state college and studied some form of humanities (classics, literature, history, or anthropology), then went to a seminary for a master's, and then went to a different seminary for another master's.

For some students, they will stand out because they have learned specialty languages (such as Syriac or Coptic). Others will impress a committee with exceptionally high grades or test scores. Another person may pique interest because she studied in Jerusalem for a term. Or perhaps a committee takes interest in a student's degree in classics. Again, the point is to place yourself in a position that will cause your application to be noticed.

CHOOSING A DEGREE PROGRAM

It should be obvious that any doctoral program will expect that, prior to entrance, a student has completed a bachelor's degree. Additionally, in almost all cases, a master's degree is also expected, and this information has been presupposed here. However, in biblical studies, there are several kinds of graduate programs, and it is sometimes difficult to decide which one is best both for preparation and in the eyes of the admissions committee.

It is common for students in this field to consider either a master of divinity or a master of arts in some area of biblical studies (e.g., MA in New Testament, MA in Biblical Studies, MA in Biblical Languages). The decision regarding which degree program is best depends on a number of factors: time and money available to complete degrees, vocational interests, type of doctoral program of interest, and subject interests. At this stage, a few notes should be made. First, a typical master of arts is two years (full-time). Though it is focused on a particular (sub-)discipline (such as

New Testament), it is difficult to fit in all of the language and methodology courses needed in such a short time, unless one has already studied this field in depth in an undergraduate program. What ends up happening is that students choose to do two master's degrees at the same time (or consecutively) and, because some classes overlap, the total time spent is about three years. It is more likely that the appropriate skills and information can be learned in that amount of time.

One must keep in mind that applications for doctoral programs are sent several months in advance of matriculation (about six to eight months), and if one is doing only one Master of Arts, she has had only one year under her belt before writing a CV or writing sample for the academic portfolio (see the next chapter for application details). This can feel intimidating and premature.

Many students opt to earn a master of divinity (MDiv). This degree is typically longer than a master of arts (MA). However, since it is a practitioner's degree (geared towards vocational training for pastors), and not primarily a research degree, it is difficult to prepare for a PhD with a traditional MDiv. There are several ways to compensate for this. In the first place, it is imperative that electives are chosen carefully, focusing on biblical languages, exegetical methods, and the development of research and writing skills. Others, including myself, have chosen to earn a master of theology (ThM) after the master of divinity. A ThM is a short research degree that follows an MDiv and is used as a stepping stone from ministerial training to advanced academic research. While some of the courses of a ThM may resemble MA courses, they are meant to be at a level slightly higher than normal master's work. Two elements typically make a ThM distinct. First, there is often a seminar-like component where students interact and discuss advanced issues in a more doctoral-like setting. The kind of debate and feedback in such courses are intended to prepare students for the setting of the supervision meeting, doctoral seminar, and academic conference. Secondly, there is typically a strong *writing* component, often in the form of a thesis whose word count ranges from fifteen thousand to fifty thousand.

When considering final employment, some seminaries tend to hire only students who have an MDiv. This usually demonstrates the applicants' commitment to a ministry focus and shows solidarity with the majority of students of a seminary (where the MDiv is the most commonly earned degree).[19] At other places of employment (such as a university where research in religious studies in the focus), the MDiv would not be a preferred degree.

In the end, it should be recognized that, in most doctoral programs, there would be little or no bias against an MDiv, though the committee may look carefully at the coursework and observe whether the student has studied at an advanced-enough level. In some cases, it may be advised that students pursue a ThM beyond the MDiv to prepare them more suitably for the doctoral level.

In any case, I highly advise writing a master's thesis to gain the important experience of research towards composing a single piece of work that involves the defense of a unique contribution to knowledge (however modest it may be). There is no substitute for the trial-and-error skills gained by attempting to develop and pursue research questions, determining the best supportive material with clear goals and conclusions. Typically, the experience of the master's thesis will include an oral defense, which offers a crucial opportunity to experience critical dialogue and interaction on the thesis.

CONCLUSION

The journey to the PhD can be very daunting. The point of this chapter was not to turn students away from the path, but to give a reasonable set of expectations for what it would take to be competitive in the application pool. Becoming an academic scholar in biblical studies is not something one can do on a whim. At the same time, it is not necessarily an occupation reserved for the genius. A professor once told me that getting a PhD is one part brains, two parts ambition.

In the next chapter, we will discuss what the application process actually looks like and how to navigate through it.

---

19. However, according to the Association of Theological Schools, over the last ten years there has been a decrease of students earning the MDiv (-14 percent), and an overall increase of students earning professional/academic MAs (+11 percent); see Association of Theological Schools, "Transitions: 2017 Annual Report," 9.

3

Making the Application

The experience of filling out and sending doctoral applications can be time-consuming and exhausting. But it is also an exciting time full of possibilities and an eagerness to transition to the next level of study. In this chapter, we will walk through the stages of information gathering, the collection of materials, and the actual sending.

COLLECTING INFORMATION

There was a time, not too long ago, when one had to order academic catalogs in order to find the right application information. Now, of course, everything is online, and for some schools this includes sending in materials electronically. The websites of the various institutions normally have all the information you need to know: the "where," "when," and "what" of doctoral applications. Once you log onto the website of an institution, typically you need to navigate to its information about "schools" (e.g., the "graduate school"). Quite often, this information can be found under the heading "academics." Once you have located the appropriate school or department, you will need to find the relevant division (e.g., religion, theology, biblical studies). Then navigate to the area that involves "admission(s)." Often a "Frequently Asked Questions" section will furnish you with the additional information you need.

FIXED DEADLINES VERSUS OPEN APPLICATIONS

Doctoral programs follow either a fixed deadline or open application system. Most American programs have a fixed deadline, where applications are due sometime in the winter, normally between December 1 and January 31 (about seven to nine months prior to the month of matriculation). Thus, if you wanted to study beginning August of 2020, you would apply in December of 2019. It usually takes about two months to review the applications, though sometimes it is longer. One can expect to receive a response somewhere between the middle of February and the middle of April.

Some programs, especially in the United Kingdom, do not specify particular deadlines, but it is wise to follow the approximate timetable of those schools that do. You want to offer ample time for a committee to thoroughly review your application materials. In fact, there is some wisdom in applying early for schools with no fixed deadlines, as they will be making a decision on your portfolio without the pressure of comparing it to dozens of other applications already received. For those kinds of schools, I suggest sending the application about nine months in advance.

APPLICATION MATERIALS

Aside from the form where you fill in personal details, the application package/website for most schools includes a combination of the following items: cover letter or statement of purpose, curriculum vitae,[1] references, transcripts, writing sample, research proposal, and test scores.[2] The first five items are almost always required, while the last two depend on the type of program and its particularities.

Cover Letter/Statement of Purpose

A cover letter or statement of purpose is an essay that introduces the applicant to the admissions committee members. Such statements must meet the institutional format and length requirements if they are specified.

---

1. The CV is the standard term in academia for "resume" or "dossier." *Curriculum vitae* is Latin and means "the course of [one's] life."

2. Additionally, some applications require the submission of a passport-sized photograph. Some programs also require proof from the student of the availability of personal funds to demonstrate the ability to pay tuition fees.

Typically, they are between two to five pages. Normally some guidelines are given with respect to what kind of information should be included. Here are some sample questions: *What do you want to study at this institution? Why do you want to study that subject area? What experience do you have in that area? What are your plans beyond the PhD?* The readers of these statements are looking for topical interest and competency, academic maturity, clarity of thought and expression, and that you are indeed a good match for their institution and program. A basic outline of a statement of purpose might look something like this: (1) the development of interest in a particular field, (2) a short background of education and advanced coursework, (3) current research (e.g., topic of master's thesis), (4) wider interests in the same field, and (5) the suitability of the prospective program for advancing educational and vocational goals.

Keep in mind the importance of demonstrating "fit." At this stage, it is inadvisable to cut corners. Try to learn as much as you can about the ins and outs of each institution to which you are applying and tailor the statement to highlight how you would be a worthwhile contributor to their community. As with any of the writing-driven elements of the application process, have a professor or doctoral student proofread and review your statement.

Curriculum Vitae

In many ways, your CV is a snapshot of your whole (academic) life. There are numerous ways to break the information down into various categories. At the stage of applying for doctoral programs, I worked with essentially eight categories. First, I listed my "Educational Institutions." Then, "Professional Experience," which included information like being a research assistant or a teaching fellow. Third, I listed relevant "Other Occupational Experience." This is useful if you worked in an academically-related environment. Next, I provided the details of any "Awards/Grants/Scholars." After that, I offered my "Language Proficiency," listing the number of credit hours taken in each one. It can also be useful, if relevant, to list "Membership" in scholarly societies. It should go without saying that there are many advantages to being a member of the Society of Biblical Literature or American Academy of Religion. I had also provided a category called "Publications," which was comprised of a few book reviews. Finally, I listed my "References."

Avoid the temptation to exaggerate information. Everything in your CV should be factually correct and accurate. Also, aim for brevity and be concise. Information should be well-organized, consistent, and easy on the eyes. A careful use of bold and italicized type styles can help certain groups of information to stand out. Again, have peers and mentors proofread your CV. A sloppy one can easily be discarded, regardless of the impressive content.

References

How to choose references was discussed in the previous chapter. In terms of requesting a reference, make sure your request is polite and that you do not assume that the person will say yes. Also, state up front the time frame that you are working with, especially when the application is due. If the referee is required to mail in the reference, it is polite to provide him or her with a stamped envelope with the address already filled out. The referee will also need to know whether the format of the reference is open (unspecified), particular (i.e., a particular form should be used), or guided (where specific topics should be treated and questions answered). In terms of timing, I suggest that you give the referee well over a month's notice (six to eight weeks). Also, it is acceptable to encourage the referee for confirmation that she has received the request, and also confirmation that the letter has been sent. If you have not received confirmation two weeks before the recommendation is due, it is acceptable to send a brief and friendly email "reminder." Nowadays, references are completed on program websites, which makes the turnaround time fast.

Transcripts

Transcripts are records of your higher education that can be obtained by each institution upon request. Doctoral applications require transcripts from every school from which you received a degree, even if your course of study is not yet complete at the time of application. These records outline each of your courses, course grades, your overall GPA, and your status (e.g., "in progress" or "degree completed"). Admissions committees are particularly interested in two things. First, they wish to confirm that you have, in fact, completed the courses of study you note in your CV. And, second, they will want to closely inspect the courses taken and grades.

When it comes to sending transcripts, your previous institutions should have a process set up on their webpages for electronic delivery. Expect a small fee. If it is financially possible, I would encourage you to keep five to ten printed transcripts on hand. Some of them you might give to your referees to help them write their recommendations. If you are applying to several programs and will not be using the same three to four people for recommendations, you may need to distribute several transcripts to your various referees. I suggest beginning to order transcripts as early as the summer before you are intending to apply.

Writing Sample(s)

A good writing sample is important to any application portfolio for doctoral studies. It divulges a number of things about the application: clarity of thought and expression, attention to detail, knowledge of area of specialty, ability to find relevant and respected primary and secondary sources, demonstration of ancient and modern language proficiency, and ability to develop and defend an argument.

The required length of a writing sample differs from one program to another, but you can expect that most will have a ten-to-twenty-page expectation. It is very important not to transgress the page range limits that are specified, as this may void the application. Keep in mind that committee members have to read dozens and dozens of these samples. This can be an onerous task if each applicant decides to submit a longer essay. Use a sample that fits comfortably within their specified range.

What should you use as the writing sample? It is standard to use an essay from an advanced course or a portion of a master's thesis. In terms of the former, it is profitable to demonstrate the ability to work through an argument, rather than simply to "comment" on a biblical text. What that means is that "exegesis" papers that describe the background and flow of a text may not showcase your skills in crafting an original argument. As for using part of a thesis, this is highly recommended, as you will have done a significant amount of research that can be seen in the essay. It is imperative, though, that the sample is reworked in such a way that it makes sense without having read the whole thesis.

If an essay or thesis portion is not ready at hand, I might recommend writing an exegetically-driven argument focused on a specific pericope. All at once, you can show language skill, acquaintance with major reference resources and commentaries, and the development of an argument that is cogent.

Again, much like any of the other parts of the application, proof-read the work several times. Typographical errors and infelicitous turns of phrases can present the critic with good reason to dispense with your application.

Research Proposal

For those programs that focus solely or primarily on the research project (i.e., dissertation), it is common to require a research proposal at the time of application. Some programs do not offer clear guidelines on the format or length of the proposal, but in most cases, it need not be more than three thousand words (unless otherwise specified).

The proposal, of course, will outline the topic that you wish to study and how you will go about researching it. It is helpful to begin with the problem or with specific research questions which will set forth the *need* for a new study. Then, the proposal could progress to previous solutions and approaches (approximating a literature review). Next, the hypothetical new direction or approach can be presented. The proposal should end with a bibliography of the essential monographs, essays, and journal articles that relate most closely to the subject. In the bibliography, it is not necessary to list reference resources like commentaries and dictionaries. Also, be sure to include non-Anglophone sources (e.g., French and German) and relevant contemporaneous primary texts. However, for the latter, be as specific as possible. Do not just list Philo or Josephus, for example, but those particular texts that deal more directly with your issue.

It is imperative that the research proposal demonstrates original thinking. It is not enough to suggest that you want to study "justification in Romans" or "the purpose of sacrifice in the Old Testament." You must prove that you have already become enough of a junior researcher to know the ins and outs of your field and know what ground has been well-worked and where more digging can be done with profit. At the same time, I would shy away from making an open-and-shut case. Keep in mind that you are suggesting that you will study this topic for a few years. Claiming to have all the answers before even starting the program can come across as naïve at best. It is better to expose the problems in the current field, suggest a potential direction, and craft a few excellent research questions that will guide the study.

In the current state of biblical studies, it is probably not enough to just want to study a particular biblical passage. I often tell prospective doctoral students that "the magic is [often] in the method." That is, many of the most significant dissertations in biblical studies derive their importance from the employment of a specific method (e.g., subcategories of areas like social-scientific criticism, rhetorical criticism, linguistic theories, narrative criticism, postcolonial criticism, etc.). Oftentimes, learning from research *outside* of the world of biblical studies brings new insight to our scholarly fields.[3]

In the British system, it is not uncommon for a prospective doctoral ("postgraduate") student to contact a potential supervisor and see if he or she would be interested in overseeing the research project. The supervisor, of course, could not guarantee admission before the full application was submitted, and the decision would ultimately fall into the hands of committees. However, sometimes that initial contact helps to match up the student with a supervisor so that, if he or she is admitted, the link is already in place. In some circumstances, the potential supervisor could give some feedback ahead of time. At other institutions, though, this kind of coaching or early discussion is frowned upon.

Should you tailor a research proposal to the interests of a potential supervisor? Yes and no. In the first place, you want to make sure that what you choose to research will sustain your interest for several years. Choosing a topic because you want to study with a particular professor is risky. What if he leaves the institution to teach somewhere else? What if she shifts her interests to another part of the field? Additionally, your topic should arise from your own background and coursework. If it does not, that will weaken your application. On the other hand, it is probably beneficial to pitch your proposal in such a way as to demonstrate that your interests relate to or complement the current interests of the faculty members.

---

3. In the past, I have recommended books such as Peter Berger and Thomas Luckman's *Social Construction of Reality*, George Lakoff and Mark Turner's *Metaphors We Live By*, Mary Douglas's *Purity and Danger*, Clifford Geertz's *Interpretation of Cultures*, J. L. Austin's *How to Do Things with Words*, and James C. Scott's *Domination and the Arts of Resistance*.

Test Scores

At the end of the computer test for the GRE, you are able to list graduate institutions to which you want to submit your scores. In terms of *when* to take the test, it is wise to consider that you may want to take it more than once.

CHOOSING A SUPERVISOR

In some contexts (especially in the United Kingdom), where the program is focused solely on the dissertation, the decision regarding where to apply is bound up closely with potential supervisors. How does one select a good supervisor? As a caveat, it should be noted, again, that it is difficult to guarantee, even if you are accepted to study at a given institution, that you will in fact work with the person you expect or desire. Nevertheless, the decision to apply to a particular program is often done with the hopes that you will be able to study with him or her, and sometimes that can take place.

One way to choose a potential supervisor is to look at the top scholars in the field of interest. One might look at the steering committee members and chairs of the conference units of the Society of Biblical Literature or the conveners of the groups of the British New Testament Society (or the Society of Old Testament Studies). Another avenue is to look at your own library and consider those scholars that have most inspired you in your field of interest. However, it is a common misconception that the best author makes for the best supervisor. One can too easily misread someone's personality based on their writing. For example, someone can come across as very friendly, social, and easy-going in print, but the story may be different in one-on-one personal interaction. Another problem is style of supervision. Just from reading an author's monograph, it is almost impossible to know how closely they supervise, how much feedback they offer, how they handle conflict, how much time they spend with their students, and their overall temperament. There are a few ways to determine some of these matters. It is always advisable to visit the school in which you are interested and attempt to meet up with the potential supervisor (with a good deal of advanced planning). Another option is to try and set up a meeting at a conference (such as SBL). If all else fails, you could contact current or recent students of that professor and ask their opinions on the kind of supervision, though each person comes to the program with different experiences and expectations.

FINANCES AND SCHOLARSHIPS

In general, you could break down doctoral programs into two categories: funded programs and unfunded programs. The former are ones where the school waives tuition and offers a modest stipend (ten thousand to twenty-five thousand dollars per year[4]) for almost all of their students. Some schools fall into a middle position, where some students receive a doctoral fellowship and others do not. The first-tier American schools tend to have fully-funded programs for most, if not all, accepted students. Alternatively, British universities and American evangelical seminaries tend to have limited scholarships.[5] Typically, students without institutional funding find income from a variety of means, including but not limited to: personal savings, part-time employment, income from a spouse, aid from friends and relatives, loans, and third-party scholarships. One third-party institution dedicated to students in religious studies is the Foundation for Theological Exploration (FTE). FTE supports ethnic minorities pursuing doctoral degrees.[6] Some church denominations have resources to support theological education. For example, A Foundation for Theological Education offers the John Wesley Fellowship, which is awarded to "gifted United Methodists in their doctoral studies."[7]

APPLICATION OUTCOMES

As mentioned above, for fixed-deadline applications, the normal time of decision is February through April. Sometimes programs work with a two-stage system, where an initial group of applicants is invited to come for a campus visit and continue the process of consideration (often involving interviews).

The best scenario is to receive an unconditional acceptance letter. However, on some occasions, programs will place conditions on the offer. This may involve the student sitting for a language examination, or perhaps it is based on the final GPA of a current degree in progress. Another

4. It is possible at many schools to receive a fellowship worth more money if it involves teaching or research assistance to professors.

5. Again, the exception is Wheaton Graduate School, which currently offers a modest stipend to doctoral students.

6. Visit their website for more information: http://fteleaders.org/grants-fellowships/c/doctoral-fellowships-for-students-of-color.

7. Foundation for Theological Education, "About the Fellowship," para. 2.

scenario may involve an offer that places the student in the doctoral program, but only on a probationary status. For instance, the condition may be that the student must maintain a certain GPA in the first year of the doctoral program.

What if you are accepted to more than one program? This would be a great problem to have! Keep in mind that offers are usually time-bound—you must accept within a certain period. This may put the pressure on as you are waiting for replies from other schools. Also, it is considered poor practice to accept an offer from one school and then, upon receiving an acceptance letter from another school, back out. In some cases, you will simply have to accept the earliest offer. If you are in the fortunate situation of deciding on two or more options at the same time, there are a number of ways to discern which is best for you. Elements such as prestige of school and faculty are usually significant factors. The amount of financial aid is also an important consideration.

What if you are rejected from all the programs that you applied for? Again, from the beginning, it is prudent to apply broadly to a number of programs—certainly the highest ones on your list, but also ones that may seem more second- and third-tier. The key is to have *options*—the more places applied, the more options. The choices must be made carefully, as money and time (of you and your referees) are involved. However, applying to only one (or only a few) programs may be risky. A comforting thought may be that, it may not be that you are unsatisfactory, but that most schools can only select a small percentage of their applicant pool (sometimes less than 1 percent). For first-tier schools, the odds are heavily stacked against the individual applicant.

The option to try again the next year should be considered. I would judge carefully, though, before simply submitting the exact same application to the exact same schools. Consider whether you may have something better and/or new to contribute: higher test scores, a published article, another language or skill, etc.

CHECKING YOUR ONLINE PRESENCE

When I was considering doctoral studies—more than fifteen years ago—I wasn't really concerned with looking into what admissions committee members could find about me online. There wasn't much there, and social media had not yet taken off. Now it is a whole other story. You can just assume you will get googled. I advise you to investigate what information is available about you online. Certain things are fine, and perhaps even beneficial (e.g., awards, honors, accomplishments), but there may be private matters that you want to make sure are private. In terms of social media, most companies have settings that ensure privacy.

Over the years, students have asked me about the phenomenon of academic "blogging"—is it helpful for getting into a doctoral program? The answer, in my opinion, is no, it is not helpful. In fact, it can be a liability. Some scholars have an overall negative impression of bloggers and blogging. They feel it is whiny, self-assured, self-indulgent, etc. Others who may be more neutral or even positive towards blogging might still feel that it comes across as too self-promotional for master's students. It is probably better to play it safe and not identify with the religion/biblical studies blogging enterprise until later.

Having offered that cautious approach, I think there is a pathway for doing *some* academic blogging. If you feel the desire to blog for personal benefit, I would encourage you to write a blog for an academic institution, such as a seminary or graduate program (where you are or were a student). Because institutions are concerned about what gets promoted from their website—and linked to their reputation—there is some professional curating that usually takes place.

The above comments about not blogging are in relation to academic and religious studies. Personally, I think it is fine if you have a personal blog that pertains to a hobby like cooking, cycling, fishing, etc. The broader concern here is that your online presence will reflect what is in your application—that you are professional in your approach to academics.

CONCLUSION

The application period is often a time of mixed emotions: anxiety, excitement, exhaustion, and anticipation. The key is to plan far enough in advance that, when the time comes, each stage of the process can be completed with minimal stress and difficulty.

SUCCEED

4

Orientation to the PhD and Choosing the Research Topic

I still remember the elation of receiving the offer to study at the University of Durham. It was not my first offer, but it was the one for which I was anxiously waiting. However, the feeling of relief and comfort rather quickly subsided and I was left with this question: *What do I do between now and the beginning of the program?* The offer letter usually doesn't have a reading list or a set of preparatory assignments.

Of course, some accepted applicants will still be finishing their master's degrees, perhaps the master's thesis in particular. It is fine to devote attention to finishing strong in the current degree program before looking ahead. Others will try to earn some extra money before diving into the PhD full-time.

There are a number of ways to occupy one's time (other than moving!) while waiting for the program to begin. Before making specific suggestions, one should take some more time and become acquainted with what it means to do a PhD—the goals and expectations.

What is a PhD? The PhD offers the highest level of education in any given academic field and prepares the person for advanced research in that discipline. In terms of skills, the one who holds a PhD is proven to be an expert in a specific area of knowledge, and also has worked toward making a new contribution. The type of original work can be understood in a number of ways, but it must clearly be "original." As mentioned before, some types of programs consider this to be sufficiently accomplished in the writing and defense of the dissertation, while others put additional value in coursework and examinations alongside the dissertation.

The expectation for a coursework-and-dissertation program is that the student will pass his or her coursework at an appropriate level of excellence. Comprehensive examinations must be passed as well. Finally, the dissertation must be written in an appropriate style, length, and manner, and defended to the satisfaction of the examiners. For the dissertation-only program, obviously, the writing project itself is the center of focus.

There is no need to worry about these things all at once. It is better to concentrate on the degree one step at a time. In the interim between acceptance and matriculation, it is helpful to gauge where you are and how you stand as a new PhD student. Each student goes into the PhD with different expectations and differing qualifications and experiences. You could probably identify your own weaker areas (and some may be quite obvious). In the next section, I will make some suggestions as to how to spend the "meantime" productively.

BECOMING A DOCTORAL STUDENT

Languages

Whatever the kind of doctoral program, language proficiency and development is fundamental, whether it is Greek, Hebrew, German, French (or Latin, Aramaic, Syriac, Akkadian, Coptic, etc.). To secure the primary ancient languages with which you are working, consider trying to read through parts of an advanced primary text. It could be a biblical text, like the Greek LXX text of Isaiah, or an early Jewish text from Philo. The more you read, the more comfortable you will become with the language.

The same advice goes for reading modern French and German. After the initial work of learning grammatical forms and concepts, one can help make it "stick" by working through a text. Many theology students find it useful to read through parts of the Bible in German or French. This is especially useful because one can compare an English translation for help, and also because some familiarity with biblical stories and terminology make it a bit easier. Also, the kind of terminology one will find in a modern German or French translation of the Bible will likely occur in scholarship.

Another option is to take a seminal article in German or French and translate it. Or one could find a trustworthy and well-respected commentary and translate that portion which relates to your area of interest. For New Testament, this could be done, for example, with an article from Ernst Käsemann; for Old Testament, Gerhard von Rad.

Knowledge Base

One expectation of the PhD student is that he or she is well-read and up-to-date on the key ideas, debates, problems, and contributions in their field. How does one develop further in this area? One recommendation I would make is to read journal articles regularly and get a pulse on what scholars are discussing. Certainly one should stay current with the most eminent journals (see chapter [x-ref]), but in particular I would suggest reading articles in your field of interest from *Currents in Biblical Research*. For New Testament studies, a new volume called *The State of New Testament Studies* (edited by myself and Scot McKnight) will come out in 2019. The *Cambridge Companion to the Hebrew Bible/Old Testament* (edited by Stephen B. Chapman and Marvin A. Sweeney) and *The Cambridge Companion to the New Testament* (edited by Patrick Gray, expected 2019) are also important volumes for staying up to date on biblical scholarship. Sheffield Phoenix Press published several volumes in a series called "Recent Research in Biblical Studies" between 2008 and 2017 on individual topics such as feminist interpretation in the Hebrew Bible, the major prophets, slavery in the Bible, and historical Jesus scholarship.

Another area of development is methodology—becoming familiar with advanced forms of analysis of the biblical literature. Earlier I mentioned how to become acquainted with basic types of exegesis and the most common interpretive approaches. At this stage of becoming a doctoral student, it is worthwhile to pursue more approaches and to move deeper into the more common ones. Again, resources abound, but you may find a few resources especially helpful. Stanley Porter has edited a valuable guide to theory and methodology in his *Handbook to Exegesis of the New Testament*, which covers (in six-hundred plus pages!) such areas as textual criticism (E. J. Epp); linguistics (Porter); genre (B. W. R. Pearson and Porter); source, form, and redaction criticism (D. Catchpole); discourse analysis (J. T. Reed); rhetorical and narratological criticism (D. L. Stamps); literary criticism (Pearson); ideological criticisms (T. Pippin); social-scientific criticism (S. C. Barton); canonical criticism (R. W. Wall); Hellenistic philosophy and exegesis (G. E. Sterling); Jewish backgrounds (P. R. Trebilco);

the Roman imperial context (D. Gill); and early Patristic exegesis (T. H. Olbricht). I suggest also reading *Scripture and Its Interpretation* (edited by Michael Gorman), which is more up-to-date on twenty-first century methods of interest including Latino/a hermeneutics, theological interpretation of Scripture, missional hermeneutics, etc. Finally, I would recommend the mature reflection on the state of New Testament studies by Markus Bockmuehl entitled *Seeing the Word: Refocusing New Testament Study*.

Critical Thinking Skills

One of the greatest obstacles in making the transition from master's student to doctoral student is learning how to engage in mature and profitable critical discussion at the doctoral level. Critical thinking skills involve not only hearing and understanding an argument or proposal, but also analyzing it and judging its validity, strengths, and weaknesses. This requires the move from being a "passive" listener/reader to an "active" one. This is not a skill you learn overnight, nor is the knowledge of it packaged into one theoretical book. It comes by observation, practice, and life experience. There are, though, some contexts that you may place yourself into to deepen these skills.

In the first place, I believe that one can grow in the area of critical thinking by reviewing books (see further [x-ref]), especially monographs. Writing a book review involves reading a book, detecting its thesis or hypothesis, and discerning whether or how well it is worked out with proper evidence. If you are not ready to write a book review, it is also useful to *read* good book reviews. When searching for very thorough and reflective reviews, there are few journals better than *Catholic Biblical Quarterly, Journal of Theological Studies*, and *Review of Biblical Literature*. Again, when reading these reviews, pay careful attention to how the reviewer assesses the book.

Another avenue is careful observation at conference sessions. Pay special attention to those sessions where there is ample question-and-answer time or where there are invited responses. It is on such occasions where you can see good critical interaction: What kind of argument did the presenter make? What did she argue? How did she prove her thesis? What did the respondent see as the weakness of the argument? How did the response develop? Can you think of other areas of weakness? What did the presenter leave out? Was any of her information inaccurate?

History of Interpretation

It is a common complaint that younger research students in biblical studies are so buried in "recent" scholarship that there is little awareness of key secondary texts written before 1980. One of my professors used to say that before taking his course on Paul and his interpreters, his students seemed to assume that Pauline studies began with E. P. Sanders and the "New Perspective on Paul." (I must confess, it was not until his course that I seriously read Rudolf Bultmann and Karl Barth.) However, the astute scholar-in-training must have a serious appreciation for how his or her discipline has been shaped by scholars over the years, whether for good or detriment. A nice place to begin is with the *Dictionary of Major Biblical Interpreters* (edited by Donald K. McKim), which includes scholars from the early church, through the Middle Ages and the Reformation, down to the present time. For more discipline-specific suggestions, you may wish to request suggestions from your own thesis advisor or future doctoral faculty members.

For New Testament studies, there is the three-volume *History of New Testament Research* (from "deism" to Bultmann) by William Baird. Also, a briefer treatment can be found in Stephen Neill and N. T. Wright, *The Interpretation of the New Testament 1861–1986*. More specific to disciplines, such as the historical Jesus, James D. G. Dunn and Scot McKnight edited a book called *The Historical Jesus in Recent Research*, which includes reviews of the contributions of Schweitzer, Bultmann, Cadbury, Kähler, Jeremias, Chilton, Meier, Kümmel, Caird, N. T. Wright, Sanders, Dale C. Allison, Borg, Stuhlmacher, Theissen, F. B. Meyer, and Robert Morgan (among others). For Paul, there is Wayne Meeks and John T. Fitzgerald's anthology *The Writings of St. Paul*, and more recently you can look at the *Blackwell Companion to Paul* (edited by Steven Westerholm), which includes a number of essays devoted to key interpreters of Paul throughout history. For Old Testament studies, one might consult Rudolf Smend's *From Astruc to Zimmerli: Scholarship in Three Centuries*, which offers brief reviews of scholars such as de Wette, Gesenius, Wellhausen, Duhm, Gunkel, Noth, and Seeligmann.

Another general resource worthy of mention is the series *A History of Biblical Interpretation* (2003–present). The first volume (subtitled *The Ancient Period* and edited by Alan J. Hauser and Duane F. Watson) treats the approaches to hermeneutics within the Hebrew Bible itself, the LXX, Philo, the Dead Sea Scrolls community, the targumim, Rabbinic Midrash, the Jewish Apocrypha and Pseudepigrapha, the New Testament authors, the Apostolic Fathers and apologists, Augustine, and the Gnostics. The second volume (edited by Alan J. Hauser, Duane F. Watson, and Schuyler Kaufman) handle *The Medieval through the Reformation Periods*, beginning with Gregory I and moving up to 1800. The third volume (edited by Hauser and Watson) covers *The Enlightenment through the Nineteenth Century*.

CHOOSING A RESEARCH TOPIC

Depending on the type of PhD one is pursuing, the decision regarding a research topic will come either before the application or actually during the program. Perhaps, then, it is best to handle the matter here in this chapter that deals with the space between application and program. Inevitably, some students will utilize this information at an earlier stage, and others at a later one.

In the movie *A Beautiful Mind* (2001), disturbed genius John Nash attends Princeton University as a graduate student in Mathematics. One of the problems he faces is the struggle to discover a "truly original idea"— the same challenge that faces any PhD student. What can I discover that is "new"? While the search for originality should become a stimulating and maturing endeavor, there is really no need to become anxiety-ridden over making the next "big discovery." Every admissions committee member or potential supervisor knows what it is like to be confronted with this problem and opportunity, and what is generally expected is the *potential* for an original contribution to knowledge, even if it is a modest one. In fact, there is sometimes something naïve or foolish in the pursuit of a paradigm-shifting proposal.

When considering a dissertation topic, there are three major elements to hold in mind (and in balance): originality, manageability, and feasibility. Originality, again, means that the thesis or idea brings something new to the discussion. One should not exaggerate what constitutes originality. In some rare cases, a researcher comes up with an idea that is so peculiar and refreshing that it completely redefines the field. I don't believe you'll meet very many who have done that! Good research is based on a reliance on primary and secondary sources, and the original contribution is found in how the researcher carries existing work forward or in a different and in-sightful direction. This can happen in a variety of ways: using a methodology from another field, comparing two texts on the same subject that have never been brought together into discussion before, giving very close and exhaustive attention to a widely neglected term, phrase, idea, etc. I often find it helpful to look closely at the assumptions about a text or event and reflecting on the real evidence for these assumptions. Sometimes these assumptions truly have a solid foundation, but in some cases they do not.[1]

Secondly, a topic must be chosen that is manageable (in terms of time and effort). One must look at the constraints of a program and ask, could I complete this study reasonably in three years (or whatever time frame given)? If someone wanted to study the concept of maturity in the New Testament, they might decide, once some preliminary research is undertaken, that the scope is simply too wide. It might be more manageable to focus just on the Gospels or on the letters of Paul (or just one Gospel). Quite often, a dissertation covers the scope of one book of the Bible. However, even that may prove too difficult, so it might be narrowed down further to, for example, Isaiah 40–66 or Matthew 5–7. Manageability could be about more than just how much text to cover. If one desired to study patterns of the use of natural elements in the Gospel parables, the topic could be further limited to just arboreal language if necessary. As for my own research project, I found that it would be too unwieldy to study all of the apostle Paul's cultic metaphors, so I chose to limit it to those in the undisputed letters, and only his non-atonement cultic metaphors.

Finally, the topic should be feasible from a research standpoint. That is, it must be a subject for which there is enough primary and secondary material in order to make a cogent argument and provide sufficient evidence. For example, on the topic of the authorship of Hebrews, while there have been a number of possible proposals for this person, it appears that there is too little evidence to prove a new (or old) hypothesis. Or, if one were making a suggestion for where Paul was and what he was doing during his "hidden years," it appears that any theory will stand on a thin layer of uncontroversial evidence.

Where does one begin to look for ideas? I offer here a few suggestions. The first is to become an expert in your field of interest. Read the most important monographs, the key textbooks, and those weighty articles that come from reliable journals and respected scholars. The more you become acquainted with the issues, perplexities, and problems in your field, the more you will begin to see "gaps" where a study is needed. Commentaries

---

1. A noteworthy explicit example of this is found in Paula Fredriksen, "Mandatory Retirement: Ideas in the Study of Christians Origins Whose Time Has Come to Go," *Studies in Religion* 35.2 (2006) 231–246.

can be very stimulating in this regard, not so much for what they *say*, but what is often left *unsaid*. Also, read broadly *outside* your area of interest— e.g., if you are a "Paul" person, start to read books on 1 Peter or Revelation or the Gospel of Luke. If you are a Pentateuch enthusiast, read monographs and journal articles on wisdom literature (for example). It is often the case that some advancement in a field foreign to yours can generate ideas for applying that same kind of method or perspective. For example, there is much discussion right now about the genre of the Gospels and determining their intended *audience*.[2] Much of the concern over methodology in audience analysis involves mirror-reading the Gospels and learning about the author, audience, and setting based on clues from the text. Much of this kind of discussion about appropriate methodology for "mirror-reading" has taken place in Pauline studies for the last three decades or so. Bringing some of that reflection into the discussion of the Gospels has recently started to take place and is ripe for fresh insight. Oftentimes, though, new ideas can be generated by reading outside of the Bible completely, and outside of traditional boundaries of biblical studies. For example, from a methodological standpoint, there is much that is being learned from advancements in ritual studies, cognitive linguistics, the sociology of knowledge, modern continental philosophy, semiotics, theories of drama and performance, social identity theories, and psychology. One place to get a sense for how newer methods have influenced biblical studies is to start paying attention to past and current issues of *Biblical Interpretation*, a journal that "provides a vehicle for the exercise and development of a whole range of newer techniques of interpretations."[3]

Another outlet for fruitful exploration is contemporaneous ancient texts. With the improvement of critical editions, up-to-date and accurate translations, and even the launching of non-biblical commentaries by biblical scholars, it is a good time to study parallel texts, whether from ancient Mesopotamia, Greece, or Rome. For example, for New Testament studies, consider working through Plutarch's *Moralia* or the sophistic and oratory writings of Aelius Theon. Or, alternatively, one might spend concentrated time in the Dead Sea Scrolls or 1 Enoch. It happens very often that ideas

2. See Bauckham, *Gospels for All Christians*.

3. See www.brill.nl/ and search in the catalog for "Biblical Interpretation." A more biblical-genre specific set of resources for exploring methods can be found in the T & T Clark Approaches to Biblical Studies Series, which normally includes a book section on critical methods.

and inspiration are sparked from thinking outside of the box and bringing two people or texts into conversation.

In terms of where in the biblical text to work, you are encouraged, of course, to let your own interests and curiosities guide you, but it should be noted that there are a number of texts that are severely neglected. While, throughout history, New Testament researchers have given a great deal of attention to Paul and the Synoptic Gospels, there is a renewed interest in recent years in James, Hebrews, 1 Peter, the Gospel of John, Acts, and Revelation.

When it comes to the type or style of the research topic or proposal, I have benefited from the basic taxonomy explicated by D. A. Carson. He proposes that, generally, there are two kinds. The first kind arises when a researcher starts with a fresh idea and wants to test it out on the material (a *deductive* approach). The second kind comes when a student looks at the information and evidence in a certain area of interest and does not begin with a firm hypothesis or presumed outcome or solution (an *inductive* approach). Carson points out that the advantage of the deductive approach is that the work is interesting and can be proven or tested easily. The problem is that, "unless the student takes extraordinary precautions and proves to be remarkably self-critical, the temptation to domesticate the evidence in order to defend the thesis becomes well-nigh irresistible."[4] And, for the inductive approach, the advantage is that the results tend to be more "even-handed," but they may amount to little more than "a lot of well-organized data."

In my opinion, most dissertations in biblical studies tend to be inductive, focusing on shedding more insight on a particular exegetical problem, fleshing out the meaning of a term or concept, or exploring a theme in more detail than before. Such studies are perfectly good and useful contributions to scholarship and become excellent reference works for students and researchers. Deductive studies are a gamble and, thus, less common. However, those dissertations that have set off bombs in the scholarly world tend to be deductive precisely because they stand against some traditional (or tacit) position and are argued persuasively. A fine example of an inductive study is Reider Aasgaard's examination of Pauline siblingship language in *My Beloved Brothers and Sisters! Christian Siblingship in Paul.*

---

4. See Carson's review of Chris VanLandingham's *Judgment and Justification in Early Judaism and the Apostle Paul.*

As for deductive studies, many are exemplary; good examples would include R. H. Gundry's Sōma *in Biblical Theology: With Emphasis on Pauline Anthropology*. Another important deductive monograph is Brian Rosner's *Paul, Scripture and Ethics: A Study of 1 Corinthians 5–7*.

As a final caveat, I wish to encourage you not to obsess over trying to stick with the first idea that you discover or work on. It is not unusual to either find that someone else has already explored that area sufficiently or that it is a dead end. Modifying a hypothesis in process is not only acceptable, but can sometimes show the integrity of following the trail of where the evidence naturally leads. In some cases, the whole thing may need to be abandoned, and you might be surprised to know how many scholars eventually gave up on their original topic in pursuit of a different one.

PREPARING FOR THE FUTURE

Some students may be under the impression that, during the PhD, the most important things are getting good grades and writing a good dissertation. While this is certainly necessary, these are not particularly the most important factors for getting a job afterwards in an academic institution. Alongside excellent performance in courses and research for the dissertation, potential employers will also be looking for teaching experience, published articles, and active participation in guild events like giving a paper at a conference. Doctoral students should have this in mind from the first day of the PhD, as it is prudent to think about these things early on and, for example, write course essays with a view towards publishing them and/or publicizing their ideas at academic meetings. While chapters 5–6 will focus on the dissertation, chapter 7 will address those other marks that define a "scholar" and shape them especially in view of future employment. Practically speaking, don't wait until the end of your PhD to read chapter 7.

LOOKING AHEAD

The next chapter deals directly with how to go about writing the dissertation, with suggestions regarding the process of research, common fallacies and challenges, and working through the whole project in a timely fashion. Under normal circumstances, there is no reason a manageable and feasible topic should take more than a few years of full-time research.

5

Doctoral Exams and Dissertation Work

R egardless of the kind of PhD, the most significant part of the process
tends to be the dissertation. In many programs, the majority of the
time is spent in the researching and writing of the dissertation. Writing
a long and substantial piece of research in the humanities is both an art
and a science. In this chapter, our goal is to give some guidelines for how
to progress through this task. Advice is given, both on a general level and
specifically with regard to research in biblical studies. Some programs,
especially in America, have required doctoral courses and comprehensive
examinations. We will begin with a brief discussion of the exams, and then
devote the remainder of the essay to the dissertation work.

DOCTORAL EXAMINATIONS (MARCUS JERKINS)[1]

Doctoral comprehensive exams evaluate the breadth of your knowledge
of the field. These exams test what you have learned during coursework
and in self-study. The dissertation gauges, on the other hand, your depth of
knowledge. In most programs, these exams represent the capstone for the
coursework portion of the doctoral journey. Once you have finished with
exams, you are now ready to proceed to work on items for the dissertation.

---

1. This section on doctoral examinations was graciously written by Marcus Jerkins,
a doctoral student at Baylor University. Jerkins offers some general information, but
presents his specific experience at Baylor.

Programs require students to take these exams to assess the student's ability to contribute to the academy. Programs are looking to see if students are capable of handling massive amounts of information and are then able to reproduce it in a way that demonstrates proficiency in handling the material. For example, is the student able to learn the scope of what is going on in Second Temple Judaism, learn what scholars past and present say about it, form her own opinion, and say something intelligible about all of this data? Fruitful scholarship can touch on all of these issues: knowledge of the subject, the history of interpretation of the subject, and how we might present new approaches to or assessments of the subject.

Typically, these exams are a series of prompts/questions. These prompts/questions are on major subjects in biblical studies, New Testament theology, archaeology in the Ancient Near East, etc. They also occur over several days. At Baylor, students are often assessed over a two-week period every other day or so. Each day the student is given several hours—I had five—and is given two to three prompts/questions. The specific prompts/questions are unknown to the student until the day of the exam. She will have spoken to her advisor about the subject from which each prompt/question will be drawn in most cases. But the student will not have any idea of the prompts/questions. In my program, we were given all potential prompts/questions that might be asked at the beginning of coursework. There were six possible questions for Day 1 of the exam, seven for Day 2, and six for Day 3. I had to be ready to respond to any of prompts/questions in essay form. Mine were closed book exams. Other programs may ask students to use books to assist in developing responses during the exam. Beyond the written exam, there may be an oral exam. Students may be required to write essays and then defend their essays orally.

Your preparation should begin with discussions with students, those who have already passed exams, and then professors in your program. I mention students first because they give the best insight. Students have taken the exams. Having been on the receiving end of the exam, they will know what it takes to pass. Also, one will want to ask them about prior questions that have been asked on exams. This may help determine the professors' tendencies. They may not ask the exact same questions, but they may ask something that is close to what they have asked before.

One should also seek counsel from professors. They will not want you to feel at ease about the exam, so they may be nebulous and evasive. The best approach is to ask them for reading lists. The book lists will help you determine the essential knowledge base for preparation.

Second, pay attention to what you discuss and read during coursework. You are bound to cover many of the topics that will be addressed during exams, like a lecture on the history of interpretation. Keep those notes. Even if the particular subject will not be addressed specifically on exams, it will help you in identifying the major voices in the field.

When you write papers, keep track of your arguments and the sources that you used. The fast-paced nature of coursework and the haggard condition you will be in after taking a class will make you want to move on as soon as you are finished writing. But make sure to keep up with what you have written. The ideas that you generated will be helpful in allowing you to form opinions on broad issues. The sources that you used for writing papers will help you so that when you begin preparing you are not starting *ex nihilo*.

As you get closer to actually taking the exam, make good use of theological reference works. Theological dictionaries and encyclopedias give you a firm grasp on major subjects in the field. These works will inevitably include discussions of major voices. You will need to know these voices.

You should try to begin studying at the beginning of coursework. Realistically, given the strain you will be under, try to use your summers as study periods. Read the major works. Memorize essential dates. Possess a working knowledge of ancient and modern figures and concepts.

Try to write detailed outlines on major topics. In my experience, since all prompts/questions were given, I was able to write an outline on every prompt/question that might be on the test. Each of my outlines ranged from three to four thousand words. They included the essential information on subjects that could be quickly reproduced in essay form. The outlines were long enough to allow me to write a detailed, evidence-filled essay. If you do not have the prompts/questions, an outline will still be a useful means to synthesize what you know on subjects so that you can quickly write on them.

I went into the exam dreading the experience and resenting the fact that I had to take it. On the other side, I must say I am glad for what I learned in preparation for the exam. I am also grateful for what I learned about myself when I took the exam. Those grueling days taught me that I have what it takes to be a scholar. I believe you will come to learn that about yourself as well.

DISSERTATION: KEEPING IN MIND THE BIG PICTURE

Before rushing off to the library or sitting down to write, it is important to think about the purpose of the dissertation, and also how it will be assessed. What is expected from you is a solid piece of research that sustains the argument of a particular thesis. Once the main proposal has been devised and stated, what remains should focus singularly on the defense of that argument through logic and appeals to supportive and illuminating primary and secondary texts. The dissertation is examined, in print and in person, on the basis of the clarity of the argument, originality, the use of clear and relevant research methods, and the appropriation of solid evidence.[2]

While researching and writing your dissertation, I suggest you keep a few "voices" in your head. Of course you will want to ask yourself how your supervisor(s) will respond to your arguments and evidence. Alongside the voice of your supervisor, I also propose you keep two others. First, have the voice of a respected "like-minded" scholar—someone that has influenced you positively. From time to time, ask yourself, *how would she respond to this chapter? Where might he look for further evidence?* Perhaps more importantly, it is useful to have a "well-informed skeptic" in your head as well. It is easy to get so caught up in your own ways of thinking that sometimes it is necessary to consider whether the thesis statement and evidence would stand up before a variety of scholars in your field. This "skeptic" will hopefully cause you to ensure that you have dealt with various things that, otherwise, you may have simply assumed the reader would accept. Occasionally you may need to ask a polite skeptic to read parts of your dissertation to help you determine your own blind spots.

Again, many pitfalls can be avoided by having a handful of people in mind as you write—scholars on a range from friendly to antagonistic. In the end, it is rarely the case that an examiner will be flat-out hostile, but it is prudent to write in such a way as to cover all your bases, both for your defense as well as looking ahead to presenting the dissertation as a published monograph.

TIMING AND RESEARCH

If you do not have time-management skills, diligence, and the good sense to know when to move on from section to section, time can quickly get

---

2. On this subject, more will be discussed in the next chapter.

away from you, and you will end up working on your research project for longer than you bargained. Some programs have checkpoints built in to aid students in managing their time and progressing efficiently in their research. In more traditional programs, the student is truly an independent researcher and is wholly responsible for imposing deadlines and working sensibly towards completion.

Of course, follow whatever schedule and suggestions provided by your program guidelines and supervisors. But if you are on your own, here are some suggestions. If you have approximately three years to complete your dissertation, though it may seem like a long time, many students don't find it to be long enough in the end. I suggest breaking the years down into three parts.[3]

In the first year, take the time to study up in your general field and become conversant with all the major books and articles. There is no reason not to read up on your dissertation topic, but the focus should be on learning the ins and outs of your discipline. If the area of your dissertation involves a close study of something in Genesis 1–3, read up on the whole field of Pentateuchal studies. If it is on the Sermon on the Mount, get acquainted with scholarship on the Synoptics. Too often, the complaint regarding PhD graduates in biblical studies is that they are *over-specialized*, lacking general knowledge. Also, part of the examiners' duties is to gauge how knowledgeable a student is in the field in general, and whether they can draw relevant connections between findings in the dissertation research and other issues in the field. That should not mean that writing should not take place in the first year. One of the most important techniques for improving writing is, simply, to practice writing. Thus, the first year is especially important in terms of refining research questions and narrowing and sharpening the thesis statement (alongside the continuing reassessment of originality, manageability, and feasibility).

If time permits, perhaps in the second half of the first year of full-time research, time can be taken for thorough exploration of primary ancient-world contextual and parallel literature. Also, a few months should be spent in the first year reading about methodology and discipline-specific methodological issues.

In the second year, one can turn attention to the biblical text and work with the primary and secondary sources in detail. I have spoken with

---

3. My view on this has been shaped, in part, by the very wise advice on dissertation writing from Phillips and Pugh's *How to Get a PhD*.

a number of commentary writers who have struggled with the question of whether to consult secondary sources at the same time as doing one's own work on the primary biblical text, or to do so after. The advantage of consulting others is that they may direct appropriate attention to terms and ideas that will come alive to you as you engage the text, and perhaps you will see a fuller picture of things as you translate and interpret. The downside of previewing the secondary literature is that your bare instincts will be, to some degree, shaped and perhaps even tainted by the history of interpretation and/or the hermeneutical lenses of others. On the balance, most recommend doing *some* initial independent work on the biblical text first to get a clean first impression. At this stage, you might translate the main text (and its wider literary context) or perform some grammatical and discourse analyses. Then the process may develop in a dialectical fashion, repeatedly alternating from individual work, to secondary literature, back to the text for testing, and back again to other writers, and so forth. Again, the practice of writing down ideas and developing short essays or sample chapters is important for processing information "out loud" (on paper or on the computer) and enhancing the skills of communication.

The third (or final) year is obviously when one does the most writing. A significant amount of time, though, will involve revising, editing, and (re-)formatting. Because the process of the examiners reading the dissertation can take some time, if you want to be finished with the whole process, the dissertation will need to be finalized sometime towards the middle of the third year.

WHERE TO BEGIN A DISSERTATION?

A dissertation typically has five standard parts: introduction (with research questions and thesis statement), literature review, methodology, main arguments, and conclusion. One of the challenges of beginning the dissertation process is deciding where to begin. It may seem logical to start with the introduction (as it falls at the beginning of the written dissertation), but a good introduction (and conclusion) can only be written accurately and cogently at the end of research when all the material has been assessed, the problems in scholarship identified, and the true contribution of the dissertation discovered.

Your supervisor may suggest a particular route to pursue, based on your topic or by experience, but if not, I would recommend beginning with a review of literature or the methodology.

Literature Review

A good review of literature presents a critical summary of the most salient and pertinent pieces of research in your field—ones that have had the most influence and brought the discussion to its present location. To begin with, select a dozen or so monographs and key articles that fit this profile and write something like a long book review on each one. Once you have done that, ask questions like: *What techniques and insights brought about some of the advancements in this area? Which perspectives and arguments have stood the test of time? Where does the most amount of disagreement lie?* In the end, you will tailor your review of literature to concentrate on the specific topic of your dissertation. What kind of information would an uninitiated generalist in your field need to know to catch him or her up to understand the state of the disciple and how your research builds on, challenges, and advances forward from where the field is currently?

Your literature review will inevitably change—perhaps even grow or shrink in terms of items covered—as you progress. You will need to revisit the question, from time to time, of the relevance of the texts in the review, as well as the issues you raise. You will also need to constantly be on the lookout for new monographs and articles that directly address your subject matter.

Methodology

Some students choose to begin their research by refining their knowledge of critical methodologies that may enhance the project. This is especially the case when the project is driven by the insights of a particular approach, whether it is social-scientific, rhetorical, linguistic, or otherwise. It is helpful to read theoretical books outside of biblical studies and have a handle on the most influential theorists within that general method's field. For example, in Richard B. Hays's now classical work on intertextuality in the letters of Paul,[4] he drew significantly from the work of the literary critic John

---

4. Hays, *Echoes of Scripture.*

Hollander and his book *The Figure of Echo: A Mode of Allusion in Milton and After*. Sometimes, the methodological techniques and principles will need to be reconceptualized or remodified to fit the context of the discussion of biblical data.

RESEARCH IN BIBLICAL STUDIES

The task of researching for a dissertation can be daunting. There are so many resources to work through in a limited amount of time. Here I will provide some guidance regarding how to go about doing research, where to look for information, and what to do with it.

Where to Find Information

Let's say that in the course of your research you will need to look at priestly language in the book of Revelation. Where do you look for good secondary resources? One route would be to open a commentary and follow the discussion. Few commentaries, though, will offer significant interaction that will point you to other sources and authors. Nevertheless, it is worthwhile to mention which ones will be most useful. The Word Biblical Commentary Series is especially helpful in that each pericope receives a separate bibliography tailored to the issues in that passage. This is also true for the Anchor Bible and Sacra Pagina. Similarly, there are a number of dictionaries that provide useful bibliographic information: The *Anchor Bible Dictionary*; InterVarsity Press's "black" dictionaries (*Dictionary of Jesus and the Gospels, Dictionary of Paul and His Letters, Dictionary of New Testament Background, Dictionary of the Later New Testament and Its Developments*, etc.); *Theological Dictionary of the New Testament*; and the *New Interpreter's Dictionary of the Bible*.

There are a few kinds of books that serve as annotated indexes and bibliographies for specialized subjects. Brill has excelled in this area with highly acclaimed indexes on Philo, Jesus research, Christ and the Gospels, the apostle Paul, 1–2 Thessalonians, 1 Peter, the Peshitta of the Old Testament, and the study of the New Testament in general.[5] Less thorough but still extremely useful is the IBR Bibliographies Series, which include sepa-

---

5. Many of these indexes appear in the series New Testament Tools, Studies and Documents (edited by Bart D. Ehrman and E. J. Epp).

rate books on *Luke-Acts and New Testament Historiography* (Joel B. Green and Michael C. McKeever), *Old Testament Introduction* (Edwin C. Hostetter), *New Testament Introduction* (Stanley E. Porter and Lee M. McDonald), *Poetry and Wisdom* (Peter Enns), *The Synoptic Gospels* (Scot McKnight and Matthew C. Williams), *The Pauline Writings* (Mark A. Seifrid and Randall K. J. Tan), *The Pentateuch* (Kenton L. Sparks), and *Prophecy and Apocalyptic* (D. Brent Sandy and Daniel M. O'Hare).

It is sometimes more profitable, though, to utilize electronic resources for in-depth research, especially as print ones become outdated very quickly. Perhaps the most useful resource is the American Theological Library Association (ATLA) Religion Database, which offers an index of thousands of journal articles, book reviews, books, and essays in all areas of religious research, including biblical studies.[6] Most institutions that have doctoral programs in biblical studies will have access to the ATLA database. Searches can be done on keywords and can be restricted by year, type of literature, or a number of other options. Sometimes, ATLA will facilitate the delivery of an article or book review via PDF download. Similarly, useful information can be obtained from New Testament Abstracts (NTA), which can also be accessed online through hosts such as EBSCO.

Sometimes, when attempting to find relevant books on a subject of interest, it is worthwhile to search a library catalog of a major university (which is bound to have volumes not in your own library). I often search Harvard University's HOLLIS catalog.[7] To complement that search, I also tend to look at the items in the library of the biblical studies research facility in Cambridge (England), Tyndale House.[8]

Finally, Google Books (books.google.com) offers access to literally millions of books. Google offers the ability to search the text of many of the books that have been scanned into the database. Though it is not always possible, on many occasions you can read the section of the book that you are looking for or the pages and chapters that contain the keywords. This is often a crucial resource because significant discussions may take place in a book which, judging by the title, you would have not assumed or guessed.

---

6. www.atla.com.

7. https://library.harvard.edu/hollis.

8. See http://www.tyndale.cam.ac.uk/. One also might consider a search on World-Cat (www.worldcat.org), which "connects you to the collections and services of more than 10,000 libraries worldwide."

THE USE OF SOURCES

General Notes

It is one thing to find good secondary resources, and another thing to put them to good use. One common problem in academic research is a misunderstanding of the purpose of supportive material in an argument. One manifestation of the problem is the use of quotations from secondary sources. Generally, there appear to be five reasons for quoting. First, a quotation is helpful when you wish to use the language of another author because it is well-written, articulate, or poetic. Sometimes it is just the case that another writer captures what you want to say in an elegant or succinct fashion. Second, the quotation may be used because it is well-known or representative of a viewpoint. For example, one might find reason to quote Albert Schweitzer's well-known line about the historical Jesus: "He [Jesus] comes to us as one unknown, without a name as of old, by the lakeside."[9] Thirdly, a quotation may be useful if it is particularly shocking or controversial. Fourthly, quotations will become important if you are extensively working through the scholarship of a particular person, especially if you are evaluating the work and desire to be careful to give an accurate portrayal.[10] Finally, if you want to cite an authority on the matter, quotations can be helpful. The temptation sometimes, though, is to stack up quotation after quotation to "show" your research. This can come across as pedantic. In actuality, being able to paraphrase the work of another shows analytical skills and demonstrates that you really understand that person's point.

Use of Commentaries

The student in biblical studies will undoubtedly find much material in commentaries, and the use of good reference works is perfectly acceptable. However, one must be aware that an over-reliance on commentaries is problematic. While decades of a researcher's work have sometimes gone into an eminent commentary, there are a number of others that were completed rather quickly with more cursory research. That is not to devalue the work of the latter, but one must assess on a case-by-case basis the utility of a commentary as evidence and support for doctoral-level research.

9. Schweitzer, *Quest of the Historical Jesus*, 403.
10. For a good example, see Vanhoozer, *Biblical Narrative*.

Some of the most respected English New Testament commentary series are the Anchor Bible, Hermeneia, the International Critical Commentary, the New International Commentary on the New Testament, the New International Greek Testament Commentary, and the Word Biblical Commentary.[11] In German, I recommend the following series: Das Neue Testament Deutsch, Evangelisch-katholischer Kommentar zum Neuen Testament, Kritisch-exegetischer Kommentar über das Neue Testament, and the Theologischer Handkommentar zum Neuen Testament.[12]

Working with German and French Sources

Good scholarship in biblical studies will, out of necessity, involve attention to relevant non-English sources. German research seems to be especially important, both in terms of the history of the development of biblical research, as well as ongoing critical discussion. French probably comes next, but some works may also be in Italian and Spanish. Sources in foreign languages, again, can be found through ATLA, as well as bibliographies in good commentaries. The Hermeneia Series, because the volumes have a more continental flavor, may be particularly helpful.

One place to look for key contributions in your area of interest is good German and French journals. As for the former, consider *Biblische Notizen*, *Biblische Zeitschrift*, and *Zeitschift für die neutestamentliche Wissenschaft und die Kunde der älteren Kirche*. For French, note *Ephemerides theologicae Lovanienses*, *Études théologiques et religieuses*, and *Revue des sciences religieuses*. Some journals consistently publish a variety of articles in English, French, and German. Three good examples would be *Biblica*, *Novum Testamentum*, and *Early Christianity*.

It obviously takes a good amount of time to feel comfortable translating German for biblical research. While some authors and works are more straightforward, others can be more onerous. It is important to invest several months, if not years, into learning the grammar and a critical mass of vocabulary of the language. As mentioned in an earlier chapter,

11. For Old Testament study, many of the same series have good Old Testament volumes, but one might also consult the JPS Torah Commentary, as well as the Continental Commentary Series.

12. French commentary series are less common, but an especially useful one is Commentaire du Nouveau Testament.

spending time in Germany or France could help you to build your language proficiency.

Nevertheless, students will vary in their comfortability and capability. Fortunately, there are a number of useful print and electronic resources to aid your translation work or double-check your own reading. For looking up vocabulary, I recommend *Cassell's German Dictionary*. Most students, though, will turn directly to the internet. For an online German-English dictionary, I suggest LEO (dict.leo.org); for French, the Cambridge Dictionary (https://dictionary.cambridge.org/dictionary/french-english/). Sometimes, though, more help is needed, especially in terms of translating a challenging phrase or clause. Though this kind of aid should not become a crutch, at times one can consult an online translator. Keep in mind, though, that the translations given by these online programs are often very rough and vary considerably in accuracy. I have found Google Translate (translate.google.com) to be particularly consistent in providing accurate translation help in German; for French, also consider Deepl (https://www.deepl.com/translator).

When you actually use the German or French research, you must be careful to cite the information correctly and interact with the resources more than superficially. A few years ago, I was challenged by the words of Markus Bockmuehl: "Rare is the scholar who bothers comprehensively with the key international publications, in part because many (formerly) distinguished institutions no longer insist that their graduate students acquire competence in the leading ancient and modern research languages. Where an author's foreign-language citations are both few in number and strikingly long in the tooth, it is hard to resist the uncharitable suspicion that they have been 'recycled.'"[13]

NOTES ON ACADEMIC STYLE

If your department does not give strict style guidelines, you may need to decide for yourself how to organize items like notes and bibliography. Generally, footnotes are preferred over endnotes, as the reader can immediately turn their eyes to the source. In America, in particular, it is also a wise choice to follow the guidelines of the *SBL Handbook of Style* (2nd edition) because it is used by so many journals and publishers, and it works out nearly every item imaginable in detail.

13. Bockmuehl, *Seeing the Word*, 35.

The key, regardless of style choice, is *consistency*—the whole dissertation must be uniform in style. The decision over which type to use, therefore, should happen early in the stages of writing to minimize the time for revision later. As for the use of footnotes, they appear for three reasons. First and foremost, footnotes are used to cite supportive documents. Secondly, they can be used for important supplementary information, such as the translation of a foreign quote or additional information regarding the issue under discussion. A third reason that some researchers use footnotes is to discuss related, but not essential, information. Sometimes this can be overdone and distract the reader, so it should be done only occasionally.

Given these reasons, you may desire to place additional information in the footnotes in an earlier stage in the process of writing and then consider cutting down the footnote material if the final dissertation exceeds the word limit. By overloading the footnotes and not the main text, even if material from the footnotes needs to be cut later, the main text can remain intact.

FURTHER NOTES ON ORGANIZING THE DISSERTATION

When it comes time to piece together the dissertation, some items should be kept in mind. First, individual chapters should be relatively freestanding and stand as an independent contribution to the overall argument. At the same time, each chapter should fit smoothly with the one before and after. Chapter lengths will inevitably vary from one work to another based on the personality of the student and the subject matter. All things being equal, though, shorter chapters are easier for a reader to digest. If it is necessary to have a long chapter (e.g., twenty-five thousand words), using subdivisions to break it down even further will give the reader opportunities to stop and reflect on the argument. Also, the titles of the subdivisions will offer the reader a panoramic perspective on the chapter.

It is not always recognized by doctoral students how important introductions and conclusions are. When it comes to academic works, introductions should be concise and clear. The introduction should draw the reader into the field under discussion and set up the research problem(s) and questions right away. Particularly when you are undertaking a deductive study, the thesis statement should appear in the introduction. Even when undertaking an inductive or thematic approach, one can preview some of the critical judgments that will be made and clue the reader in to the uniqueness of the approach and results of the study.

The conclusion is also very important, and care should be given to summarizing the argument well. It may be helpful to write the conclusion keeping in mind that, if and when it is published, researchers may rely on the final statements in the book to understand the contribution of the study (especially if researchers don't read the entire book). While the examiners will certainly have read the whole dissertation, the conclusion offers an opportunity to reinforce the main points of the study and the significance of the whole project.

Other things can be accomplished in the conclusion. It is important for the dissertation to demonstrate how the conclusions and contributions you have made on the very narrow subject you are studying have relevance to wider issues in your field. The conclusion could be a time to explicate (even if only briefly) what insights can be gained for other areas of study based on your own findings. This kind of exercise will also help you process how to "pitch" your dissertation to a publisher when the time comes, as publishers are very interested in reaching the largest audience possible for any book they publish.

The conclusion also creates an occasion for looking towards where your research can go in the future. This involves an awareness that your study could only take the discussion so far, and inevitably there is much more that can be explored and considered. This part of the conclusion might suggest new applications of your theory or model, or an expansion of the scope of the study. In a way, it gives researchers a way to utilize your work for future projects. The final chapter of a dissertation is a time to look back on the work, but it is also a time to look ahead—to step out of your research cubby, place your work within the context of the ongoing study of your field, and make a case for how your ideas will have a profitable impact on conversations in various other sectors of biblical studies (and beyond).

LEARNING IN CONVERSATION

Much learning in a doctoral program obviously comes from reading books and articles. However, one should not underestimate the value of face-to-face conversations with scholars and other research students. These kinds of interactions offer the ability to think out loud and also receive advice and information that is not in print. Your own graduate program probably facilitates conversation and discussion through coursework, seminars, workshops and/or local conferences. Some students choose to meet regularly for a meal and spend time discussing research. This could be formal, where a different student is chosen each week to present to the group a small part of their research during breakfast or lunch. A more casual setting would allow students to raise issues, ideas, and questions about their experience as such matters come to mind.

Writing a dissertation often inspires students to seek out the experts in a field and have meaningful conversations about the area of interest. Working with a supervisor that specializes in that field is one opportunity for these kinds of discussions. How else can this take place? Another option is to contact a scholar and attempt to meet and discuss research. This situation, though, must be handled very carefully, as a brash request could come across negatively. I offer two important recommendations here. First, seek out, before contacting the scholar, a point of connection between you and them. Do you have a mutual friend? Are you from the same state? Did you meet them once before? Are you friends with one of their colleagues? Making use of a connection will probably warm the scholar up to you, as email can be a sterile form of contact.

Secondly, try to set up a meeting with the scholar at a major conference like the Society of Biblical Literature annual meeting or the British New Testament Society Conference. This will take the pressure off of finding a time in a busy "normal" schedule to meet with a stranger. Academic conferences are often designed to accommodate "free time" where scholars can meet with friends and colleagues. You might offer to talk over a meal for which you will pick up the tab.

While I have had good success in meeting up with scholars at conferences and having meaningful discussions, there are a number of things I would suggest *not* to do. First, don't be pushy. Imagine that high-level scholars have their own students and supervisees to worry about, let alone trying to fit in one more person. Secondly, keep your emails short and to the point. Don't write a lengthy email outlining your life story and summarizing your research ideas. A busy scholar will likely glance at a long email and plan to read it later (or never). Provide basic information about yourself (name, institution, supervisor, topic) and be specific about how that scholar's work is relevant to you. Be sure to mention that you are a doctoral student—the more advanced the discussion, the more likely the scholar understands that he or she is one of the *only* people that can engage in the kind of conversations that will be beneficial to you.

Also, don't send them any written work to read on the initial email. This can seem very presumptuous. It is better to allow the first-contact email to be a polite request to meet and discuss research. If the response is positive, you can gauge (based on the tenor of the response) whether you want to ask them to preread something.

When it comes time to meet, don't make it an opportunity to impress the scholar. Remember that you are there to listen and get feedback. Be prepared with some of the ideas you want to discuss and give ample time to let the scholar respond. Also, be very mindful of the timeframe. If they say they have to leave in an hour, check in at that time and say, "How are we doing on time? I really appreciate you meeting with me and I don't want to make you late for what you have next."

As for the time *after* the meeting, again, you will need to assess whether the scholar is willing to pursue the conversation further. The post-meeting emails could lead to them reading a portion of your work, but don't assume. Continue to make polite inquiries and requests so as not to use up the goodwill of a new friend.

Finally, be careful not to crowd out your own doctoral supervisor with the voice of scholars you are in dialogue with. You may want to let your supervisor know that you are meeting with a scholar to discuss your research. Afterwards, take care not to pit this scholar's advice against the instruction of your supervisor.

COMMON MISTAKES AND BEST PRACTICES IN BIBLICAL RESEARCH

Taking a step back from the nitty-gritty of doing a dissertation, I would like to offer some general advice on avoiding common pitfalls in biblical research. Then we will offer "best practices" for how to go about constructing an argument and defending it appropriately.

Pitfalls

One common problem with biblical research is an *overreliance on commentaries*. While they are certainly important for studying biblical texts, not all commentaries are well-researched, and many of them borrow from each other often enough that it amounts to a lot of wasted time and circular reasoning.[14] A second problem is the technique of research I call *"plundering."* That is when a student comes up with an argument and then "plunders" a bunch of books and articles looking for bits of relevant information and supportive evidence. The real problem is that a page here and there is read, but the student is focused on finding a good quotation rather than really learning from and critically engaging with other scholarship. The best scholars take the time to read *whole* books and essays, understanding the shape of an entire piece of scholarship and utilizing it carefully. That does not mean that every book on the subject must be read in its entirety. Rather, it is about the attitude towards research—are you really trying to understand the shape of discussions in your field, or are you just trying to make and support your argument with text citations?

Another serious problem is an obsession over an *apologetic* or *doctrinal proof* through exegetical discussion. Some dissertations seem to be singularly focused on reinforcing a particular theological doctrine. Regardless of the motive, this can often lead the researcher to force the evidence to fit the intended preconceived conclusion. This is not a critique of theological interpretation or an appeal to some disposition of absolute objectivity, but a serious caution against studying a subject where you have vested interest in the conclusion coming out in only one way. The ideal context and method of research involves the conclusions being led by the evidence. Correspondingly, the "conclusion" must be left open until all the evidence has been analyzed.

Sometimes students make the mistake of *interacting with only one subset of scholars*. Sometimes this happens because a student prefers a certain set of scholars that are like-minded and ends up quoting the same two or three scholars throughout the study. This can come across as myopic and simplistic. Another issue involves a student showing bias against a group

14. In recent years, instances of plagiarism and lack of proper citation have emerged with regard to several academic commentaries. It is not that plagiarism is a new problem (as if it didn't happen before), but probably more so that newer technology is able to better detect overlap between two works. There is no way to know ahead of time if a commentary is reliable; but this is a good occasion to be reminded that it is important to check the accuracy of your sources, and—for yourself—make sure you cite accurately and give credit where it is due. Part of the problem seems to involve (1) clear note-taking for your research (so you can identify which are your thoughts and which are from others) and (2) training and communicating carefully with research partners and assistants to prevent any miscommunications. See "Eerdmans Statement"; Gundry, "Statement from Zondervan Academic"; cf. also Hausman, "Announcement from Lexham Press."

of scholars and, thus, ignoring their research. This can be true when "conservatives" ignore "liberal" scholarship or *vice versa*. One way to avoid this pitfall is to have a variety of scholars in mind when you are writing the dissertation and think—*How would X scholar evaluate my sources? Or what about Y scholar? How about Z scholar?*

There is a common mistake also regarding *the age of the sources*—some students get stuck in only the most recent sources and ignore scholarship that is more than twenty years old. Chances are, though, your examiners are quite aware of older relevant scholarship and will inevitably feel that you have missed out on good research. Be sure to read and interact with literature from all periods of the twentieth century, but, of course, with good awareness of the poor perspectives and presumptions of any age.[15]

One pitfall comes with *the temptation to follow rabbit trails too often*, and thus digress from the main focus and path of the dissertation. Once in a while, an excursus may be tolerable or even necessary. Also, sometimes, it is acceptable to discuss important ancillary information in footnotes. However, the main text of the dissertation should follow a smooth road from introduction to argument to conclusion in a way that the reader is not trying to guess the relevance of any particular discussion.

Sometimes students discuss related but nonessential topics out of a desire to make a contribution on every subject they have studied. However, it takes maturity and diligence to weed out material, however interesting, that does not add to the main thesis of the study.

The use of charts and diagrams can also become a problem when they are too complex or not self-explanatory. It is worthwhile to test the charts on other doctoral students to gauge whether they are clear and helpful. That is not to say that visual illustrations are not complementary and useful—when they are used well, they can be very insightful.

Finally, it may be helpful to discuss at this point the appropriate use of contemporaneous primary literature. Much of biblical scholarship involves looking at parallel literature and making comparisons and contrasts whether it is Hittite hymns, Sumerian apocalypses, Josephus, or Seneca. These kinds of horizontal glances can be paradigm-shifting and epiphanic. However, there is often the temptation to overdraw commonalities or contrasts, and then the exercise can become reductionistic. Sometimes the problem

---

15. For example, New Testament scholarship is quite different in the second half of the twentieth century versus the first half due, in large part, to the discovery of the Dead Sea Scrolls.

is an obsession with "parallels" that presume that the biblical author was trying to do or say the same thing because of some similarity with another text. Another problem is confusing "background" with "context." I believe that Troels Engberg-Pedersen's comments on this issue are instructive. Some time ago, a conference convened to discuss "Paul and His Hellenistic Background." When it came time to publish the papers into a book, the decision was made that the term "background" should not be used, and that "context" was more appropriate. Engberg-Pedersen writes, "Paul was part and parcel of Hellenistic culture, a participant in it as opposed to an outside spectator of it."[16] I find this very insightful, as students as well as professional researchers too quickly label and categorize. One way to avoid this pitfall is to work deeply and thoroughly with the nonbiblical texts. Become an expert in that group of texts, so that you are aware of the dangers of stereotyping. Similarly, the more you know about a text and its history of interpretation, the less likely you will be to overdraw comparisons and contrasts.

Best Practices

In the first place, write in such a way that you are ready for your thesis to be examined before the very best experts in your field—even the ones that you would naturally disagree with. The point of a dissertation is not that your argumentation and evidence will convince *everyone*, but rather that you have made a sufficiently plausible argument using methods and evidence that are appropriate to your field and generally accepted.

Secondly, set out to work both critically but also graciously with other scholars and sources. One must be able to point out limitations and weaknesses in the work of others, while also acknowledging a significant debt to previous researchers.

Thirdly, avoid making such an argument that the result is a strict yes or no. While sometimes you can get away with such a study, they tend to get disproven or outdated rather quickly. It is better to argue a thesis with differing levels of plausibility. Some parts of your argument can come out black and white. Other parts may be more *probable* or *suggestive*.

Finally, a good dissertation needs to be clear and relevant above all else. Clarity can suffer when the work is poorly organized and riddled with typos and errors. Alternatively, clarity can be achieved by an intuitive

16. Engberg-Pedersen, *Paul in His Hellenistic Context*, xv–xvi.

design to the study, regular breaks in reading where summaries and restatements of the thesis idea can be found, and a conclusion that wraps things up. Relevance, the "so what?" factor, may make or break a dissertation in terms of satisfaction of the research and also its longevity as a useful piece of scholarship.

WORKING WITH A SUPERVISOR

An important part of working through the dissertation is working *with* a supervisor. Every supervisory relationship is different, based on the approaches, experience, and personalities of supervisor and supervisee. Some supervisors are more "hands-on" and take an active role in crafting the project and seeing it through with the student. This kind of supervisor usually (though not always) makes a strong effort to guide students towards good sources and ideas and away from bad ones. Another kind of supervisor is more of a sounding board, wanting only to help when the student asks for it. It is not my place to dictate which type is best, and there are many different philosophies on this. The important thing to do is to be clear with your supervisor about what you want and what they want. Lay your cards out on the table and be honest about what you expect. Don't be pushy about how things should go. Many supervisors have been at it for many years, even decades. You may need to be open to new ways of learning and being mentored. The important thing is that there is an open line of communication and that problems are not buried.

If the supervisor does not bring it up, it is entirely appropriate to talk about how often you want to meet, how the sessions will go, and what you can expect in terms of feedback. One area to be especially clear on is what is expected of you by the supervisor in terms of revision. Are you expected to make changes on *anything* that he or she makes comments on? What kind of freedom is there to politely disagree? When is a comment an open question, a hesitation, or a serious concern? Without being defensive, it is acceptable to work towards establishing clarity in regard to any of your supervisory concerns.

DISCOVERING ANOTHER WORK ON YOUR SUBJECT

A final issue worth discussing is the perennial fear of graduate students— *What if you find a recently published book on the same topic?* In many cases, this is not the end of the world. Of course, you will need to get a hold of the book and see just how close it is. In a deductive study, you will need to discern if they have a similar enough proposal to yours to warrant a redirection of your own research. It is possible that this could happen, but unlikely. If your study is more inductive, the chances are much lower that the conclusions and evidence of the other book is nearly identical.

If the other study is very similar, one route would be to modify your study. This could involve changes to scope, comparison texts, methodology, etc. In some ways, though, it could be a good thing for a study to appear—it shows the importance and interest in the same topic. Also, the other book may make a nice dialogue partner. Finally, you may find that the other study points to sources that you may have never thought of and that would have been hard to come across otherwise. A good thorough reading of the similar work will probably attune you to the weaknesses of that study, which you can discuss in your own literature review.

CONCLUSION

The work of researching and writing a dissertation is exhausting and exhilarating at the same time. Through a process of working between primary and secondary sources, and a cycle of trial and error, you will learn how to do research and how to move the discussion forward in a subset of your field.

6

How to Defend Your Work
(Preparing for Your Formal Defense)[1]

For many people, the formal defense of the dissertation is the pinnacle of the process of earning the doctoral degree. It is the last barrier to breach to make it to the other side of academia—from student to professional. Because it happens behind closed doors in many institutions, it can also be a bit mysterious and even intimidating. However, if you think about it, you probably know many people with PhDs and probably only a few (if any) who failed. That means the odds are in your favor that the system will work correctly and, if you follow the guidance of your program director and advisors, there is really not too much to worry about. Your focus should be on writing your dissertation, keeping in mind the criteria by which you will be examined. In this chapter, we will talk about the purpose of the defense, the process, the possible outcomes, preparing well for it, and strategies for getting through it.

Before turning to the defense, I would like to say a word about the final submission of the dissertation. Before you make a final printout of the dissertation for submission, you want to be absolutely sure that everything in the work is accurate and free from error. I advise that you read through your whole work at least twice. If possible, have another doctoral student

1. In the United Kingdom, the oral defense of the dissertation is called the *viva*, short for *viva voce* (living voice). For an insightful discussion of the defense process and appropriate preparation, see this website: http://www.research.stir.ac.uk/documents/SeminarNotes-VivaNotes.pdf.

read through it, looking for easy-to-spot typos and grammatical infelicities. In biblical studies in particular, special care should be given to making sure biblical citations are correct (e.g., watch out for Psalm 161 and 2 Titus 4:5!). German and French quotations (and your translations of foreign language sources) should be double-checked for accuracy. Comb through the bibliography and double-check consistency with abbreviations and correct spelling for foreign language works (e.g., proper accenting for French and properly placed umlauts for German). Greek, Hebrew, and other ancient text fonts throughout the dissertation should be checked to make sure the same fonts are used in every chapter and that they turn out appropriately on a printout.[2]

Don't forget to make an extra copy of the final product for your own use in the examination (for your reference).[3] You will want to ensure that the copy from which you work in the examination is identical in content to the ones that the examiners have. This is especially important with pagination. You don't want the examiners to refer to a certain page while you have to hunt for the corresponding material in your own copy (or vice versa).

THE PURPOSE AND PROCESS OF THE DEFENSE

Purpose

In most PhD programs (especially in North America and the United Kingdom), it is not enough to write a significant piece of research. One must also be able to defend it before experts. The defense, while explained slightly differently by each institution, tends to have five uses. First, it is a way of authenticating the work of the dissertation—*Did this student really write this?* Based on the defense, the examiners can assess whether the

2. Unicode fonts for Greek and Hebrew have become standard now because they do not require the receiver/reader to download specialized fonts. The Society of Biblical Literature offers a helpful discussion of unicode fonts and presents keyboard layouts to facilitate typing in Greek and Hebrew; https://www.sbl-site.org/educational/biblicalfonts_faq.aspx.

3. For either your penultimate draft of the dissertation (which you will look over for editing and proofreading purposes) or for the copy you will use as your personal copy for the defense, consider printing it out and binding it with the help of the self-publishing website www.lulu.com. Because it prints two-sided and works with millions of people, it could be copied and bound for a fraction of the cost of a local printing service. However, for the copies that will be submitted to the university (and go to the examiners), carefully follow the guidelines and suggestions in your program handbook.

dissertation came directly from the student. While it is probably not common to find students stealing entire dissertations from other people, a more likely danger is that the research is more the work of the supervisor or other mentors than the student. Again, though, in most cases there is little or no suspicion of plagiarism. Authentication is an important formality, and you would probably not be asked anything directly related to this (e.g., *Is this your own work?*).

A second purpose of the defense is to ensure that the student has become knowledgeable in the academic field in general. *Can you set your work in the broader context of your discipline?* In that respect, questions may be asked regarding the relationship between your very narrow study and its implications for other areas of the field. Thirdly, examiners will want to challenge you or test you on various ideas and arguments in your dissertation. This is often a time for a good academic conversation that provides rationales for the way you conducted your research and why certain choices were made.

Fourthly, the defense can sometimes tip the scale if the examiners are on the fence about whether the dissertation is worthy of passing. It can be a make-or-break time where certain clarifications and answers could encourage the examiners to give the student the benefit of the doubt. Finally, the defense can be a time where the student is given useful feedback for how to improve the dissertation, especially in the hopes of increasing the chances of publication in a good monograph series. It is during these kinds of conversations that the student really feels like a professional scholar.

Process

It may be helpful, at this stage, to walk through the process of getting to a defense. How the examiners are selected will depend on the type of institution. In the United Kingdom, one examiner comes from within the department and another examiner is chosen from outside your university or institution—usually an expert on your subject. The examiners will receive your dissertation and will have a period to read through it. In the United States, a committee is formed that will examine the dissertation consisting of several department/institution members (and sometimes a subject expert from outside of the department/institution).

In their assessment of the written work, there are usually a handful of things that they must consider. First, *does the work make an original contribution to knowledge in its field?* It is not enough to have a nice summary of scholarship on an issue or collect data in a clear manner. There must be some useful advancement beyond what already exists. Second, *is there evidence of independent critical ability*—that is, did the student interact with other scholars at an advanced level, determining strengths and weaknesses in the work of others? Thirdly, *is the dissertation clear and accurate?* Is it written coherently and without an abundance of mistakes? Is the literary presentation acceptable? Finally, some programs insist that the dissertation demonstrate suitability for publication, in part or whole. This is a matter of standards: *does the dissertation meet the guild's standards of excellence?*

In the United Kingdom, the examiners typically fill out a report independently which answers some of the above questions. Often a preliminary decision is made (again, independently) regarding the acceptability of the dissertation. At the defense itself, the examiners compare notes and determine which issues they would like to raise in the defense. At the end of the defense, the student typically leaves the room for a short period while the examiners make a final decision. The student is, then, invited back in, and the committee's recommendation is reported to the student. In the majority of cases, the recommendation of the examination committee is accepted by the graduate school and becomes official.

POSSIBLE OUTCOMES OF THE DEFENSE[4]

With such an important and complex work as a doctoral dissertation, it is hardly appropriate to leave it up to a simple "pass" or "fail" outcome. Usually, while passing with flying colors and failing miserably are certainly options, there is a range of outcomes in between. In the best of scenarios, the final decision could be that the student is awarded the degree and the dissertation is completely satisfactory "as is." This, admittedly, is rare. There is usually *some* room for criticism and expectation of improvement. But there are many other kinds of positive outcomes. First, you may pass with only minor corrections. This is usually a confirmation that the dissertation is accepted on the condition that some changes are made here and there to word usage, phrasing, and unclear information. Under such circumstances, this does not involve a trip to the library for further research. It is something that can be done in less than a month's worth of work.

---

4. You should consult your own program handbook for details concerning the possible outcomes. I offer here general comments on what many schools do.

Less ideal, though not completely hopeless, is the examiners' proposal that the dissertation undergo major revision. Usually, in this instance, the work has serious potential and makes a contribution to the field, but is not acceptable as it stands. Perhaps a chapter needs to be reworked or another chapter written that fills a lacuna. Sometimes it is judged that a certain kind of evidence or line of reasoning is unjustified or improperly employed. These kinds of changes, as they are more substantial, often require more research. There is usually no guarantee, once the changes are made, that the dissertation is worthy of acceptance. The examiners will explain how the process of assessment will happen after the changes are made. Sometimes the examiners will simply reread the work and make a decision. On other occasions another defense will be necessary. It is important that the student clearly understands what kind of changes are expected, the timeframe, and how the dissertation will be evaluated at the end. This can sometimes seem like a nightmare scenario, and it is certainly not a pleasant experience, but I have known people to have found a silver lining to this kind of dark cloud. Some students who have found themselves in this situation have, in the end, felt that such changes strengthened the work for publication. Certainly some may feel that the examiners were unfair, but, in the end, they are the final arbiters.[5]

The worst-case scenario is that the examiners may decide that the work is not worthy of a PhD. This kind of outcome should not really be an option for most students. The reasons why this sometimes happens is that students don't follow the guidelines of the program and dissertation handbook, misunderstand the nature and purpose of a dissertation, consistently disregard the advice of the supervisory team, and/or rush through the research work.[6] Perhaps the most common reasons are the last two. A student may feel that the supervisor is not available enough, difficult to work with, or not necessary as a mentor. Usually, the vices here on the student's end are fear or hubris. A responsible student, though, will address any concerns directly with the supervisor. If you want to meet more often, it is within your rights to talk this over with him or her in a respectable

5. It is, of course, possible to contest the final decision of the examiners as unfair, but such cases are relatively rare. Please consult your handbook carefully on these matters if you desire to pursue such a course of action, and talk it over thoroughly with your supervisor or program director beforehand.

6. It is also possible that the problem is with a stubborn and highly-opinionated examiner, but the reason why there is more than one examiner is to prevent bias against the opinions and work of a student.

way. Also, one must keep pride in check, as the temptation may be to ignore the suggestions for changes. It may be helpful to know that at many schools, supervisors regularly go through workshops and training seminars on improving their role as a research mentor. The lone ranger student who tries to do it all by themself does not really model the skills of a good researcher, who collaborates and dialogues with others to fine-tune academic capabilities and test ideas.

As for time, whether it is because money is running out or a student has taken a job, finishing the dissertation prematurely can have disastrous effects. Examiners can often tell when a student has just thrown the last three chapters together and slapped on an introduction and conclusion. Remember that having to undergo major corrections and revisions may take many months.

Again, it is very unlikely that you will flat-out fail, if you have carefully and patiently worked through your research under the guidance of a good supervisor. To add an extra measure of caution, I recommend you ask your supervisor directly, when you think you are done, whether he or she thinks you are ready to submit the work for final consideration. Again, it is not the supervisor's place to ensure you that you will pass, but a green light to submit from the supervisor may give you extra confidence.

Another measure of comfort comes in knowing that it is usually the case that the defense helps you pass. Alternatively, if the examiners find the dissertation acceptable, it is unlikely that they will decide *not* to pass you based on the defense (unless they question whether it is your own work). The best way to feel ready and confident for the defense is to believe that your dissertation is your best work and meets all the expected standards of originality, clarity, publication worthiness, etc.

PREPARING FOR THE DEFENSE

Knowing what the examiners will be looking for in the written work and also how the defense will be assessed is a large part of getting ready for the actual examination. Obviously this affords you time to think about the contributions you have made to scholarship and why your work is worthy of acceptance by the institution. You may want to reflect on and even write down (to help you clarify) your research questions, your thesis statement and hypothesis, a brief description of your methodology, a broad description of your evidence, the logical flow of your dissertation, and the results.

The best way to prepare for the defense is to know your own dissertation from cover-to-cover. Take some time to go back through the work and get a sense for what is there and where various pieces of information are. You may want to memorize the chapter breakdown of the dissertation, and maybe even the subdivisions within the chapter, so that you can speak knowledgably about the dissertation when the time comes. Though the examiners will have read the work carefully, they may have forgotten that you did in fact handle an issue they raise. If you know your work well enough, you can point directly to that spot when the time comes.

Because you may be asked to give a summary of your thesis, it is useful to take some time and memorize a two-minute version of it. Also, have a longer version ready as well (e.g., an eight-to-ten minute version). The process of writing the abstract for your dissertation (which usually appears in the front matter of the work) is a good exercise in this regard.

Some programs have examination workshops, where special advice is given regarding the completion of the dissertation, the submission process, and the defense. It may be worth the time to attend such an event, especially if program-specific advice is given. Also, if the institution permits, try to attend a defense. The best way to demystify the experience is to witness it firsthand and see that it is not usually as harrowing of an experience as some make it to be.

Finally, one of the best ways to be ready for the defense is to set up a mock examination with your supervisory team. If that is not possible, try to do it with anyone who has read your dissertation. Have them ask you both general questions and specific questions about your research. General questions that examiners ask may include: *Can you summarize your main argument in one sentence? What are your key findings? What is original about your work? Can you tell me why you think this merits publication? What are the strongest and weakest parts of your work? Why did you select the methodology that you did? Looking back, what might you have done differently and why? What implications do your results have for your wider field?*

Your mock examiner(s) should also press you on specific questions. He or she may request clarification on issues or challenge you on your knowledge and assessment of ancillary texts (such as your use of evidence from the Old Testament Apocrypha, the Targumim, Josephus, or Rabbinic literature).

Another step to take is going back (again!) through your dissertation and making a list of further corrections of typos. Inevitably you will find more minor mistakes, and that is to be expected. It is prudent to print up a list and take it with you to the examination. If you show early awareness of these, it may suggest to the examiners that you are committed to making your work error-free.

In the weeks just before the defense, there is no use in obsessing over the upcoming experience. There is some wisdom in having a small amount of reverential fear as a motivator for knowing your work, but too much stress could backfire and cause you to lose confidence. After working through this advice, if you still have a few weeks or days left, you could do a few of the following. First, read up on the published works of the examiners. Get a sense for their academic interests and passions and what kinds of things they find problematic. You can have the expectation that they will be fair, but it is helpful to know what pet peeves they might have as well! Secondly, do some light reading in your field more generally. Don't over-exhaust yourself, but just peruse the latest journals in your field and build up your general knowledge while trying to get your mind off of the impending assize. Finally, some students have chosen to pick up a different small project to work on to busy their time. It could be a review, or perhaps a potential article related to your research.

SURVIVING THE DEFENSE

When the time finally comes for the defense, dress conservatively. It may not matter at all how you dress, but why take the chance? Also, take with you your Greek and/or Hebrew Bible (depending on your discipline), your copy of the dissertation, a pad and pencil (for writing down comments and questions), and an *errata* list if you have one.

Obviously you will want to be a little bit early. They will probably provide water, but if not, you may want to go and get a cup of water to take with you. In terms of attitude, don't go into the room with guns blazing ready for a fight. You will probably annoy or offend the examiners and get the fight you were expecting! Instead, regardless of what it may actually turn out to be, treat it like a conversation about your research between senior scholars (them) and a junior scholar (you). Pretend that you are consulting with them about how to shape up your dissertation for publication in a top-tier monograph series. This will help you to keep the process in perspective and avoid getting defensive.

You will want to greet the examiners and address them formally. The examiners will probably take a few minutes to remind you of the process and tell you how the defense will be conducted. Questions will probably go from very general to very specific (and may end generally again). Normally some "easy" questions are asked at the beginning to put the student at ease. Also, the examiners may initially make some positive comments to offer some encouragement before addressing problems and weaknesses.

In terms of the line of questioning, every examination is different, and there is no use in trying to prejudge which questions will be asked. Be prepared to write important questions down for consideration later. It is acceptable to take a bit to think about the question or to ask for clarification if you don't understand it exactly. Be careful not to over-answer the question or ramble. For most questions, you could provide a sufficient answer in just a few minutes.

You may want to write down some of the important questions you are asked, but in a way that it is clear you are actively listening to the examiner. After the whole defense, you will likely share your experience with others and spend time reflecting on it. However, you may be surprised how quickly you will forget the details of the defense. If some of the comments and questions were meant to shape the work up for potential publication, they may not offer such feedback in written form. Also, writing the questions down shows an appreciation for the viewpoints and feedback of the examiners—that you take their perspectives and concerns seriously.

One strategy that has been effective for answering questions is the "define-defend" method. When a question is asked about the dissertation, first "define" what you did in the dissertation and then defend why and how you did it. Keep in mind that you are being evaluated primarily on the work of the dissertation. It is reasonable to direct attention back to the work. It is not necessarily useful to bring published material of yours that does not appear in the dissertation into the discussion. That falls outside the scope of what they are examining.

Another important issue involves knowing when to counter-challenge a criticism and prove that your work on that matter was appropriate and when to concede that your work was limited. That is, choose your battles carefully. On some points, it is not really crucial if you are shown to be mistaken. Accepting criticism and recognizing one's own blind spots and weaknesses can be a sign of maturity.

Don't make up answers to questions on the spot if you genuinely don't know. On the other hand, you can do more than admit ignorance. I suggest dealing with such a situation in this way: "I don't know the answer to that question, but I could offer a guess." That way, you acknowledge that you are not speaking from direct knowledge, but you welcome the opportunity to think on your feet and make an educated contribution.

Don't expect to know the decision of the examiners ahead of time or at the beginning of the defense. While you may have heard stories where students received the comforting word of their passing right away, this is exceptionally rare. During the examination, don't presume that light questioning means an easy pass or hard questioning means certain failure. Suspend such snap judgments and focus on having a productive conversation with the examiners.

FINAL THOUGHTS

The time of submission and defense is exciting. On some occasions, when the student has undergone the defense and leaves the room for deliberation, the committee welcomes him or her back by saying "Congratulations, Doctor!" Of course, there is inevitably going to be paperwork, correction of further minor spelling and grammar mistakes, and a new journey towards employment, but you can be proud of accomplishing something special and admirable. This chapter, then, concludes the section called "Succeed," as its purpose is to help guide you to completing your doctorate "successfully!" If you have made it to that point now, well done!

However, the PhD is not just the end of one thing (a degree), but also the beginning of another (your academic career). In the next section ("Advance") and the chapters within it, we will explore how to transition to being/becoming a scholar in the field of biblical studies, which involves publishing your dissertation, acquiring academic employment, and starting your research and teaching career on the right foot.

ADVANCE

7

Orientation
From PhD to Employment and Beyond

Now that we have covered the essential elements of successfully progressing through a doctoral program, it is time to look ahead to the next stage—getting an academic job and becoming a professional. One cannot put off thinking about this future during the doctorate, though, because some of the factors in finding employment involve planning ahead and accomplishing a number of time-consuming tasks.

During the doctorate, it is important that the graduate coursework, exams, and dissertation remain the central focus, but especially when it comes time to search and interview for jobs, you will realize that teaching and research institutions are looking to hire someone on the basis of a number of factors. In some disciplines, it may be the case that a good dissertation and degree from a top-notch school is enough. However, especially in light of the competitive job market in the field of biblical studies, the bar has been raised at many schools.

Beyond the baseline expectations that a job candidate has a doctoral degree from a respected institution and a worthwhile dissertation, the other main considerations usually include (but are not limited to): publications, teaching experience, research and teaching interests, conference presentations, theological and denominational commitments (in some cases), and administrative experience. Of course, there are other elements that play into this equation, such as personality and personal "connections."[1]

One can better understand the gap between the work of a doctorate and the required qualities of a professor in this way. Let's take the example of a small liberal arts college looking for a new instructor. In most cases, they are not going to prioritize the qualities of an advanced researcher. Most likely, they want someone who has a solid amount of teaching experience, can fit in well with the other faculty members and administration, supports the vision and ethos of the school, and communicates comfortably and effectively with students. Reading excerpts from a dissertation, however remarkable, can hardly attest to such things.

The key, then, is to begin the doctorate paying appropriate attention to the requirements of the program, but also in view of building those skills and credentials that will most likely put you in prime place for getting ahead of the job-hunting pack. Towards the beginning of the program, it may be wise to set some non-dissertation goals and actively seek out opportunities to gain experience in some of the above-mentioned areas.

That is not to say that no PhD programs make such training and opportunities available in teaching, conference presentation, and administrative experience. There are some programs that attempt to incorporate these items. However, many programs do not or cannot, and no program will be able to offer it all.

One consideration that should be made in advance involves reflecting on what type of job you will be seeking after the PhD. Do you want to focus on a research university? A Christian liberal arts college? A seminary? In the end, most job seekers probably won't be able to be that picky, but choices you make during your graduate studies greatly affect your suitability for certain jobs. For example, undergraduate schools may be looking particularly for prospective professors that have significant experience teaching at that level. However, you may only have experience as a teaching assistant for graduate courses. While that difference can sometimes be considered negligible, to others it may be more problematic. Or a research-intensive institution may be looking for professors with supervisory experience. If

---

1. One example of "connections" involves the reality that some institutions like to hire their own alumni. This is primarily the case if one receives a bachelor's or master's degree from that institution. The desire to hire new faculty with their earlier degrees from that same institution is logical enough—it gives some reassurance of "fit." By and large, though, most schools tend not to hire faculty that earned their PhD from the same institution.

you desire to gain experience in this during your doctorate, you may ask your doctoral supervisor if you can help supervise a master's student (or, in the United Kingdom, undergraduate students write supervised theses as well). Again, when it comes down to it, you will probably have to apply to whatever jobs are out there regardless of the type of institution, but certainly you will "fit" better in some, and it is helpful to know this in advance.

FINDING TIME

Surviving a PhD is hard enough—how can one also manage to accomplish these other tasks? Where can time and energy be found? Perhaps this will offer little comfort, but it is just what is required to raise the potential of finding a professional job. However, there are ways to integrate some of these elements into the work of the PhD. For example, in terms of writing articles or book reviews, much of this work can be carried out through graduate course essays and assignments. Or, if you have too much material that you researched for a chapter of your dissertation, this could be turned into an article.

Another answer to the time question is that sometimes sacrifices are going to have to be made. When I was about to begin my PhD, I asked a friend who had recently completed his how he managed to finish early. He said, "I was single-minded in my work. When it happened to be nice weather, while other students saw this as an opportunity to have some fun outside and travel, I was in the library diligently moving forward."[2]

Through efficiency and advanced planning, you may be surprised what you can accomplish. It is important to set (realistic) goals for each year or half-year and work toward them. For example, I set out to publish about an article per year of my PhD program.

2. While I highly encourage you to be focused and resolute about your academic goals, I don't intend for this to communicate that family time and responsibilities should be limited or neglected. In fact, everyone needs an outlet to unplug once in a while and have a life outside of the PhD. Also, time with friends and family can be rejuvenating. Rather, the point here is that some doctoral programs are set up in such a way that the student sets the pace and schedule. That can be difficult for some who do not know how to pace their studies and set challenging deadlines and goals.

LOOKING AHEAD

The following three chapters will deal with the matters of publishing, conference participation, teaching experience, and job hunting in greater detail. Again, you shouldn't wait until the last minute to read these chapters or think about these issues. The sooner you get a grasp of their importance, the sooner you can work toward getting experience and placing yourself in good stead for the academic market and preparing for a fruitful career.

8

Conference Participation
and Publishing

Two clear marks of a good scholar or doctoral student are published pieces of research (articles, essays, reviews, etc.) and active participation in academic conferences (presenter, chair, respondent, etc.). Especially for graduate students, the research experience can be very isolated and have a minimal impact without attention to such avenues of dialogue and interaction. Also, practically speaking, when the time comes for the job search, a demonstration of such activity often shows that the prospective professor is a real participant of and contributor to the field of biblical studies. We will begin by discussing how to get involved in conferences.

CONFERENCE PARTICIPATION

Conferences come in all shapes and sizes and have a variety of purposes. For biblical studies, the "big event" in America is the Society of Biblical Literature annual meeting (SBLAM), which circulates around major venues in the United States.[1] This conference is divided into over a hundred smaller study groups (called "program units"), which cover nearly every subdiscipline of biblical studies imaginable from biblical books (Pentateuch, Synoptic Gospels, disputed Pauline letters, etc.), to methodologies (social-scientific, semiotics, rhetorical criticism, narrative criticism, etc.),

1. See https://www.sbl-site.org/meetings/AnnualMeeting.aspx.

to specialized topics (warfare in ancient Israel, Bible and film, Pauline soteriology, etc.).

Other meetings are more modest—for example, some doctoral programs have a yearly symposium, sometimes jointly held with another university or seminary. On some occasions, graduate students present in a group separately from the scholars. Other times, such lines are not drawn.

Besides the SBLAM, there are a few other major conferences worthy of mention. First of all, several academic groups hold their own meetings either close to the same time as the SBLAM or under its auspices. As for the former, the Evangelical Theological Society has its annual meeting usually just before the SBL conference.[2] At the very beginning of the SBLAM, the Institute for Biblical Research meets in conjunction with SBL.[3] While both organizations are evangelical, the latter one is more focused on biblical studies, though ETS does have a number of program units devoted to biblical books and topics.

Both SBL and ETS have regional meetings all throughout the United States that typically meet in the late winter and spring. These conferences tend to be rather small and excellent places for students to get experience presenting and meeting other students and scholars.

In the United Kingdom, the most popular biblical studies conferences are the British New Testament Society conference and the conference for the Society of Old Testament Studies, which meet separately.[4] Also, the Tyndale Fellowship (associated with the Tyndale House in Cambridge) holds an annual meeting every summer and is divided into "study groups," including biblical archaeology, biblical theology, Old Testament, and New Testament.[5] Finally, New Testament scholar Susan Docherty organizes a conference that meets yearly in Wales called The Annual Seminar for the Study of the Old Testament in the New.[6]

Beyond the United States of America and the United Kingdom, there are also major conferences held by the European Association of Biblical Studies (EABS), and the Canadian Society of Biblical Studies.

2. See http://www.etsjets.org/annual_meeting_overview for a description of the upcoming ETS meeting.

3. See https://www.ibr-bbr.org/ for a description of the upcoming IBR meeting.

4. Respectively, http://www.bnts.org.uk/ and https://sots1917.org/.

5. See https://sites.google.com/view/tyndalefellowship for a description of the upcoming meeting.

6. See https://www.newman.ac.uk/staff/prof-susan-docherty/ for information on Susan Docherty.

A number of other societies, oftentimes affiliated with a denomination or religious group, organize conferences such as the Catholic Biblical Association, the Society of Pentecostal Studies, the Wesleyan Theological Society, and the Stone-Campbell Journal. Though one should not aimlessly seek out membership in various groups, if you do associate yourself with a group that has a conference, this might provide an excellent opportunity to gain experience presenting your research and meeting other scholars.

PRESENTING A CONFERENCE PAPER

The Proposal

The process of presenting an academic paper begins with a good idea (from your end) and the conference "call for papers" (from their end). The call usually comes three to six months in advance (by an email list or through the conference website) and potential presenters are encouraged to make a proposal.

A proposal typically requires a title for the presentation/paper and an abstract (along with your personal information). The title should be clear and catchy. You may want to be transparent in the title regarding the texts you are going to deal with in general. One option is to make the main title a bit humorous, mysterious, or poetic, and then allow the subtitle to be more explicit about topic and texts. It is perfectly normal and encouraged to run your title and abstract by friends and mentors.

The abstract is rather more important when it comes to assessment. An abstract is meant to give the interested reader a taste of what you will be discussing. In some cases, it is appropriate to provide a summary. In other cases, you may feel that it is better to discuss the questions and issues involved, but leave the conclusion unstated to raise interest.

In terms of choosing the topic, you may want to draw from your dissertation or graduate coursework. However, try and give the topic broad appeal so that the subject seems interesting to a wide range of people. Consider the wider implications for the study of that material (hermeneutics, historical or social issues, authorship, etc.). This will certainly increase its chances of acceptance. However, be wary of aiming too broadly, as an unwieldy topic could make committee members suspicious that the subject cannot be treated in the course of a short paper.

Another important consideration is *originality*. Does the title and abstract communicate that something "new" will be offered? Make it clear that you will be driving the discussion forward by opening up a new perspective or working with fresh evidence and/or materials.

Finally, as with anything else, be absolutely sure that the proposal is completely free from spelling and grammatical errors—a sloppily written proposal will make the judgment process much lighter, as they have an easy reason to throw out one.

It may help to know how proposals are decided upon. In the first place, a committee is normally in place (as with SBLAM) to decide upon the proposals. A chair is responsible for collecting and distributing the proposals.[7] The committee then works through a discernment or voting process to decide. For the SBLAM, some groups vote based on a ranking system where each committee member assigns a score to the proposal from one to four. When the tally is made, the highest scoring proposals are placed in the open slots. Thus, the acceptability of the proposal may depend on the slot-to-proposal ratio and the composition of the committee.

Getting Accepted and Writing the Paper

Once the proposal is accepted, you should move forward and write the paper in full.[8] The organization of the paper should be like any other type of logical argument: introduction, methodology (if worthy of explicit mention), main arguments, and conclusion. One popular and effective way to begin an academic paper is to talk very broadly about a subject and then narrow in on the special issue. This eases the hearers into the paper. Another route is to start with a bit of humor. This is best done with anecdotes, not with actual jokes or puns.

In terms of length, it is often difficult to know how long to make a paper. This obviously depends on the time slot, but other factors are involved such as the complexity of the topic and the personality of the speaker. A

---

7. In most cases, the ideal is that proposals are judged based on merit and not status, so the proposals are passed along without names attached to them (i.e., "blind peer review").

8. If you do not write the paper before sending the proposal, at least sketch out the outline of the argument and ideas and think through the main books and articles that will become conversation partners. If you don't do this, you may end up not being able to logically make the arguments that you originally presumed and face the embarrassment of pulling out of the paper or redirecting the topic.

safe range to work with is to average about 100–150 words per minute. If you have a twenty-five-minute slot, you will want to aim for between 2,500 and 3,750 words for the paper. As for myself, I try to plan for about 125–130 words per minute.[9] If you have a tendency to make extra comments during a paper (that are not written), you may want to write a shorter paper.

Inevitably, I see presenters (young and old, student and scholar) try to squeeze a six-thousand-word paper into a twenty-five-minute slot. What usually happens is that the paper is read at a lightning speed (unintelligibly) or the presenter has to cut out parts of the paper on the fly (which comes across as unprofessional and choppy). A third possibility is that the chair, whose role it is to keep the papers on time, will let the presenter go overtime. However, this is impolite both for the next presenter and also for the auditors.

On the matter of communicating well to a listening audience, avoid long lists, facts, and figures. I always encourage presenters to have handouts for the attendees. It is useful to give the title of the paper, your name and contact information, a basic outline of the paper, and any key texts or information that you want them to have for reference. This is especially useful when dealing with arguments where you will make reference to Greek or Hebrew biblical texts.

In addition or instead, you may furnish the audience with copies of the entire paper to follow along. While the gain is that the participants will have the whole paper for reference later, the downside is cost.[10]

The Big Day of Presentation

In most cases, it is advisable to dress conservatively. I tend to show up to the meeting room about twenty to thirty minutes early. Sometimes it is harder to find the room than you think, and other times you may have to help rearrange furniture or set up the microphone. It may also ease your nerves a bit to visit shortly with the other presenters and the chair ahead of time.

---

9. For more on speech rate, see "What's Your Speech Rate?" The site acknowledges that speech rates vary widely. "Studies show speech rate alters depending on the speaker's culture, geographical location, subject matter, gender, emotional state, fluency, profession or audience" ("What's Your Speech," para. 4).

10. Also, some may be wary of passing out ideas that have not yet been published or copyrighted.

In that time before the seminar or unit begins, ensure that you have some water, as well as a pad and pencil with which to write. I would also recommend bringing two copies of your reading manuscript to the session, just in case you ruin one with coffee or in the rain. For extra safety, I tend to email an electronic copy to myself so that if the physical copies completely disappear, I can access it and print it at the business center of my hotel.

When reading the paper, make eye contact as often as possible, but in a comfortable way. Your voice should be clear and sufficiently loud, and you can feel free to take a brief sip of water, especially at natural breaking points in your paper.

Normally, a short time of discussion is permitted at the end of a paper.[11] Make use of your pencil and paper and write down the questions. Sometimes the audience will pick up on gaps in your reasoning or items you overlooked. In other cases, someone will point out an error in the data. It is good practice to accept criticism graciously. This can be very difficult to do and takes practice for some. However, the more open and approachable you are, the more feedback you are likely to get. If you feel threatened by a criticism or pointed question, it may help to remember that you were selected to give this paper, and you have something worthwhile to say. The question and answer time is not a defense of your paper *per se*, but should be viewed as a time for mutually beneficial discussion and one for you to find ways to improve your work.

Sometimes you will not know the answer to a question. In such cases, as with the doctoral defense, it is okay to confess ignorance. However, it is often profitable to venture a guess. Another special situation is when there is silence and no one asks a question. This can be awkward, but it does not necessarily mean that the paper was uninteresting or unworthy of comment. During such times, the chair usually pipes in with a question to prime the pump. If not, don't worry. It is not uncommon for a paper to generate few or no comments.

---

11. At the SBLAM, discussion varies and will sometimes take place after all papers are presented. A common schedule is to limit discussion to five minutes after each presentation.

PUBLISHING BOOK REVIEWS AND ESSAYS

Introduction

Publishing a book review or review essay[12] is an excellent way to get writing and publishing experience, and also it normally involves receiving the book for free![13] During a PhD, writing a book review can be a nice break from the seemingly endless task of progressing through the dissertation.[14] One reason why doctoral students choose to review books is to acquire new works in their own field, especially ones that relate to the dissertation. Occasionally, it is faster to get the book for review than to request your academic library purchase it or to have it come through interlibrary loan.

Also, I try to review books outside my own narrow field of expertise to help expand my knowledge and spark ideas that might inform my thinking. If I don't get such books to review (with deadline pressures), I tend to put such aspirations on the backburner.

Finally, I recommend reviewing books because it is a nice practical exercise in active and critical reading. When you read a book with the knowledge that you have to write something substantial about it for print, you tend to be a careful reader, looking to see what the thesis statement is and how the author(s) set out to prove it.

The Process of Becoming a Reviewer

Often, when students first consider writing a book review for print, there is the assumption that you (as reviewer) get to choose the book and then you seek out a journal who will publish it. While this is a logical assumption, there is a bit of a different system, especially for those who are just beginning. In reality, journals are not normally anxiously looking for people to

12. A "review essay" is essentially a work that lies somewhere between a standard review and an article. Sometimes, in a "review essay," the essayist will discuss several recent books (that are similar in subject matter) at once. In other cases, one book is under review, but the essayist uses the book as a case-study to discuss wider issues in the field. And sometimes a review essay is simply just longer than a normal "book review."

13. In almost all cases, authors are not paid for writing book reviews or articles (unless it is for a magazine).

14. See an encouraging discussion of this issue in a past issue of the SBL online publication called "SBL Forum": McEntire, "Why I Still Write Book Reviews."

review the important books. Oftentimes, they handpick who they want to review those kinds of books.

To help you understand where you might fit in the process, it may be useful to know generally how journals work with publishers. When a new journal is formed, typically the editor(s) will contact various publishers and request to receive relevant books they produce for review. The publisher, once it has assessed the validity and excellence of the journal, will set up the journal book-review editor (or journal headquarters) to receive regular shipments of relevant books to circulate to reviewers. Once a review on a book has been published, the publishers want the journal to send them a copy of the review to pass on to the author.

The book-review editor of a journal, then, is often receiving dozens of books, and it is their responsibility to find reviewers. It is not as helpful for the review editor if a person simply contacts her and requests to review a certain book. Also, in such circumstances, the editor cannot really be sure that the potential reviewer is a competent and reliable reviewer.

A better approach is to contact the review editor of a journal of interest, and politely request to be added as a reviewer in a particular area of interest (such as the Gospels, prophetic literature, Christian origins, etc.). The editor, then, can get back to you with a book suggestion or list of books in your field. You may or may not get a chance to review the exact book you wanted, but it is best to see this as the building of a good relationship between you and a journal. Eventually, if such a relationship is built, you can put yourself in a position where it would be more possible to request specific items.

Choosing a Journal

There are many different kinds of journals in biblical studies and religious studies. Some journals have only a few book reviews per issue, while others have many (such as *Journal of Theological Studies*). Some journals don't have *any* book reviews (*Tyndale Bulletin*). Other journals are completely devoted to academic book reviews. Three journals that you should be aware of are the *Review of Biblical Literature*, *Religious Studies Review*, and *Reviews in Religion and Theology*; all of these are "review journals."

Review of Biblical Literature (*RBL*) maintains an active list of books available for review online. *RBL* is the premier biblical studies review journal produced by SBL. It is published in print as well as in PDF files through its website: www.bookreviews.org. *RBL* maintains not only a catalogue of every book review they have published (which is nearing five thousand), but also a running list of books available for review (for SBL members). At any given time, they have hundreds of books available. The process of acquiring a book through *RBL* is unique. Once you have chosen a book you would like to review, you then need to present a short proposal regarding your qualifications for being a good reviewer for that particular text. The editorial committee may receive many proposals for the same book and will select one person based on his or her expertise and the strength of the proposal.

How do you choose a journal to work with? If you are new to this process, I suggest steering clear of the weightier journals. Start with a seminary journal or another smaller periodical. First, locate the journal's website. Then find the book-review editor's contact information.[15] Send an email to the appropriate editor giving your name, degree program (or your highest degree), a short (two to three sentence) bio, and what subject area you are interested in. Then, you may simply write, "I am interested in writing a review for your journal. Do you currently have books in my subject area of interest?"

In response, they may send you the name of a book or two, and you are free to take or leave the offer. Or, they may send a list of books and you can select one.[16]

Once Approved, the Process of Reviewing a Book

Once you have worked out with the editor which book you will review, the book will be sent out. Deadlines for book reviews vary depending on the journal. Some journals desire a fast turnaround time to ensure that they stay on top of the demand and provide the earliest reviews on a book. Typically, a reviewer has at least three months to read the book and write a review. Other journals allow for more time and offer up to a year to finish a

15. Some journals may have only one editor that covers all matters in the journal, whether articles or reviews. Other journals may have several editors, and some even several book review editors.

16. Once you have a handful of reviews under your belt, you might be able to select two or three books at once and work on them at the same time. For good reasons, journals tend to send only one for first-time reviewers. Once you have built up some credibility and your writing skills are proven, there is usually more wiggle room in this area.

review. The journal website will often contain guidelines for reviewers that should be read carefully.

In terms of the length of a review, this also varies from one journal to the next. *RBL*, for example, is quite generous, and reviews sometimes appear that are over ten pages. Generally, though, a review is about six hundred to a thousand words. *RSR* publishes short reviews of 250–300 words. Again, such matters will be stated in the style guidelines, either on the website or sent to you by email.

When it is time to write and send the review, you will need to follow the format of the journal as requested. Most journals today allow email submissions, which are more cost-efficient, easier to track, and allow the editor to reformat or edit the review easily.[17]

Advice for Reading Books and Writing Reviews

While a book review is normally a very short piece to write, and this can make it easier, sometimes it is still difficult to decide what to write about. Occasionally, the journal editor or journal guidelines will specify how much attention should be devoted to summary of the book and how much to critical interaction. Nevertheless, a helpful general format is as follows: short introduction (10 percent), a summary of the book chapters and argument (45 percent), positive feedback (20 percent), negative feedback (20 percent), and end statements (5 percent). Clearly, a major part of a review involves a fair and clear description of the content of the book, especially the thesis statement or main idea. If the book is an edited collection of essays from multiple authors, it may be helpful to list out the chapter titles and contributors.[18] The introduction of the review, like any good opening, should try to attract the reader's attention. You may want to start with a provocative question or make reference to a perplexing or controversial issue in the field that the book addresses. In the end-statements, it is profitable to give your overall impression of the book, what audience it would most suit, and its enduring value for scholarship. In terms of review etiquette, one should avoid harsh and undue criticism. In most journals, negative

---

17. It is helpful to be aware, though, that journal editors tend to not proofread the reviews as well as they do the articles, so you will want to be extra careful that your review is free from grammatical and spelling errors before submission.

18. I only do this, though, when such information is not readily available online.

feedback in reviews is welcome and even desirable, but it should be done in a professional and respectful manner.[19]

When it comes to reading the book, it probably won't be enough to simply "read" through the book and then write the review. I suggest reading it when you can take notes and in such a way that you can refer back to critical junctures in the book when you are ready to write. When you read, you will want to be on the lookout for these items: the central thesis or idea of the book, the methodology employed, the key points of argumentation (and evidence), and key assumptions. Ultimately, your readers will want to know, among other things, whether the author successfully defended the thesis statement or main argument. You will also want to look for the following: omissions (was anything left out that should have been discussed?); focus (are some areas given too much attention while others are too thinly treated?); attitude (is the author fair in their assessment of the work of others?); sources (does the author use primary sources responsibly vs. prooftexting?); and originality (is the argument fresh?).

Personally, I find that the best way to review a book and remember what I thought about it is to make notes *in* the book itself.[20] For those of you who are willing to do so, I offer here my own system for making annotations. When I read a book that I want to analyze closely, I use the same system of marking. Whenever I come across what I consider to be a main point that the author is making, I write "MP" (main point) in the margins. If I come across a statement that I might want to quote from the book (whether it is excellent or disconcerting), I write "Q" (quote) in the margins. If I come across a point that I find useful or impressive, I place an asterisk (*) in the margin. If there is a statement with which I disagree or find serious fault, I place an "X" in the margin. When there are pages which I will want to find later again (especially with "MP" or "Q"), I circle the page number, so that when I flip through the book, I can identify them quickly.

In the back of the book, I find a blank page where I can scribble thoughts and concerns, and where I can keep track of things like the number of typos or errors.

---

19. For my own good practice for each review, while I am reading the book I try to discern at least two areas that are weak as well as at least two useful items or points.

20. Some of you, I am sure, like to keep your books free from markings. Feel free to skip this section.

Advice for Reviewing Commentaries and Textbooks

One of the doctoral student's favorite items to review is the biblical commentary. However, these have become specialized kinds of resources that do not work like other books. They are reference works, and it can be a bit daunting to review one. What do you comment on? What is a review reader interested in knowing? I suggest, when you are reading the commentary, to pay special attention to the following factors: audience/depth (Who is the commentary written for and what is the intended level of depth? Pastors? Scholars? Has the author maintained consistency regarding depth and level?); originality (Does the commentary fit a niche? Is it unique enough to warrant a library purchasing it?); methodology (What is the scholar's approach to the text? Rhetorical? Historical? Other? Is it too one-sided? Is it consistent?); format (Does the commentary flow nicely? Is it well-organized?); introductory material (Is the introduction too short or too long? Does it cover the most important issues?); sources and ancient texts (Does the commentary refer to helpful sources? Does the commentary accurately interact with the biblical text and other ancient texts?); currency (Does the commentary make use of current discoveries, methodologies, and recent secondary literature?); and appended or additional items (Does the commentary offer useful charts, bibliographies, excurses, or charts?).

Textbooks are also a bit unusual to review because they do not typically have thesis statements. Some of the same areas of evaluation could apply for dictionaries and textbooks: audience, depth, format and organization, useful appendices and charts, and currency.

PUBLISHING JOURNAL ARTICLES

Introduction

One of the most important ways to improve your CV and share your research is by writing articles for good journals. While books take years to write and publish, articles are important because they are current, cutting edge, widely available, and easy for readers to consume in a short time. In fact, I suggest that a PhD student should try and publish at least two articles during the doctoral program in view of attracting the attention of potential employers when job-hunting time rolls around. How, though, do you get started in this area?

Finding an Idea

The first thing to do is come up with article ideas. These can come from all sorts of sectors. One convenient place is graduate course essays. In fact, it is wise to think ahead and write course essays in such a way as to make them "publishable." We will discuss what that means in a moment. Another place to find ideas is the dissertation. Quite often, you will end up doing more research and taking more notes than you can fit into the actual dissertation. Some "extra" material might work nicely as a basis for a good article.

Finding a Journal

There are many different kinds of journals and periodicals that one could consider for publishing an article. Some journals are associated with an organization (like SBL), while others are independent. Some come from a confessional perspective while others do not. And, of course, some are interested in a specific portion of the Bible or methodological (or ideological) perspective. Perhaps, though, the most useful taxonomy is simply one that ranks journals according to academic excellence.

World-Class Journals (in Alphabetical Order)

- *The Catholic Biblical Quarterly*
- *Journal of Biblical Literature*
- *Journal for the Study of Judaism*
- *Journal for the Study of the New Testament*
- *Journal for the Study of the Old Testament*
- *Journal of Theological Studies*
- *New Testament Studies*
- *Novum Testamentum*
- *Revue Biblique*
- *Scottish Journal of Theology*
- *Vetus Testamentum*

- *Zeitschrift für die Neutestamentliche Wissenschaft und die Kunde der Älteren Kirche*
- *Zeitschrift für die Alttestamentliche Wissenschaft*

Excellent (in Alphabetical Order)[21]

- *Biblica*
- *Biblical Interpretation*
- *Biblical Theology Bulletin*
- *Biblische Zeitschrift*
- *Currents in Biblical Research*
- *Early Christianity*
- *Ephemerides theologicae lovanienses*
- *Harvard Theological Review*
- *Horizons in Biblical Theology*
- *Jewish Quarterly Review*
- *Journal for the Study of the Pseudepigrapha*
- *Journal for the Study of the Historical Jesus*
- *Journal of Theological Interpretation*
- *Judaism*
- *Neotestamentica*
- *Religion in the Roman Empire* (2014–)
- *Tyndale Bulletin*

Very Good (in Alphabetical Order)

- *Evangelical Quarterly*
- *Journal of the Evangelical Theological Society*
- *Journal for the Study of Paul and His Letters* (2010–)

21. It should be noted that normally *Interpretation* and *Ex Auditu* would fit into this category, but I do not officially list them because they don't tend to accept unsolicited manuscripts.

- *Perspectives in Religious Studies*
- *Restoration Quarterly*
- *Westminster Theological Journal*

Other Notable Journals (in Alphabetical Order)

- *Anvil*
- *Bible Translator*
- *Expository Times*
- *Themelios*
- *Trinity Journal*

The Writing, Submission, and Assessment of an Article

When it comes to actually writing out the article, have in mind one or two journals that you are considering for submission. Download or request the style guide from your first choice and get a sense for the expectations.[22] In terms of length, the average journal expects an article that is between six to nine thousand words. Articles should be thoroughly researched, working with classical resources as well as the most recent sources. It is also expected that the article interact with worldwide research (i.e., French and German scholarship, as well as Anglo-American).

It is fundamental that the article clearly demonstrates original research. It is usually not enough to summarize a concept in a field or explore a theme. Also, use of original languages (Greek, Hebrew, and Aramaic) should be accurate and insightful. As a matter of general practice, to ensure that I have written my best work, I try to (1) read the paper (or a condensed version) first at a conference and learn from the feedback, and (2) have a colleague or mentor read and comment on the article.

Once it is time to submit the article, make sure that it is completely free from grammatical and spelling errors. Also, double-check that foreign language words are correct, especially accents. To submit an article, you normally send it to the journal editor. Consult the journal website for specific instructions.

---

22. If you are using a reference-management software package such as Endnote, you can switch from one kind of style (e.g., Turabian) to another easily.

In the email, it is helpful to include your name, whatever Greek/Hebrew fonts you are using, and provide a statement that you have not simultaneously submitted the same article to another journal.[23] Additionally, as an author, I ask for a very general idea of how long the assessment process will take. Normally, it can range between two months and one year. On average, an assessment is made in about three or four months.

Academic journals in the humanities tend to subscribe to a policy of double-blind peer review. That means that the article submission is sent by the editor to two reviewers (sometimes more) and they are "blind" in the sense that the author's name is removed from the article so as to maintain anonymity for the purpose of fairness and objectivity. Also, the identities of the reviewers are hidden from the author, with the editor acting as a go-between.

Often the reviewers come from the journal editorial board. The names of the scholars on the editorial board typically appear on the journal website to show the prestige and range of scholars for that journal. It is almost impossible, though, to "guess" who will receive your article. In fact, it is sometimes necessary for the editor and board members to send the article outside of the board for review if the subject matter requires a specialist, or if the normal board members are unavailable.

The process of review usually involves reports on the article sent back to the editor. This includes an evaluation of the originality of the article, its overall academic excellence, and sometimes a discussion of whether it fits the journal's profile in terms of method or scope. If the reviewer finds an article unworthy of publication, a list of problems is provided. In turn, the editor passes on the news to the author, along with comments. If the article is accepted, the reviewers usually have suggested or required corrections/modifications. The author is given some time to make these adjustments.

There is the possibility that the editor and reviewers are on the fence about the article. In such cases, they may request that the article be rewritten or significantly modified, and the outcome could still be unclear.

If the article is accepted and corrections are requested, the author is responsible for deciding how to edit and improve the article based on the comments. If you are unsure, it is acceptable to ask the editor for advice or clarification. There is no standard timeframe for making these

23. Almost all journals require this last piece of information as they do not want to hear back from the author that another journal has accepted the same article as this wastes the time and efforts of the reviewers.

improvements, and it would depend largely on the nature and quantity of the corrections. Typically, author and editor together would work out a deadline for corrections.

Once the corrections are approved, the article is placed in line for publication. How quickly the article appears depends heavily on the frequency of issues (bi-annually, quarterly, yearly) and how many articles are accepted in a given year.[24]

Once the article has been published, the journal will inform the author and furnish them with "offprints"—copies of the article to keep or distribute to friends and colleagues. However, as journals continue to go online as well as in print, it is becoming more common to simply receive a digital (often PDF) copy of the issue or article in lieu of a set of offprints.

Dealing with Rejection

If an article is rejected, it can be difficult and discouraging, but it is also a very common experience for scholars as well as students. I tend to work with a "three-strikes" principle of article submission. I pre-consider three journals that fit the article in terms of scope and method. Two of them are usually in the "world class" and "excellent" categories, and one of them in the "very good" or "notable" category. I send the article first to the highest category and work my way down once it has been rejected. If an article has been rejected three times, I usually table it and consider it unworthy of publication. Of course, at each level of rejection, the feedback of the reviewers should be taken into consideration, and changes should be made to improve the argument.

If an article has been rejected by a journal, it does not necessarily mean it was seriously flawed. Some journals have so many submissions that they have to be very cautious and hold to the highest standards for publication. Sometimes it is truly the case that a reviewer was biased against an idea or ideological statement in an article, but the point of double or triple review is to insure balance. Nevertheless, just because one journal deems the article "unpublishable" does not mean that another journal's reviewers will come to the same conclusion. Again, it is advisable to have a current or former professor or supervisor read the article and provide clear and honest feedback.

24. Even though the article may not appear for years, it is common for authors to list them as "forthcoming" in their CV.

Frequently Asked Questions

Can I turn parts of my dissertation into articles during my PhD? The answer to this depends on the policies of your current program. Some programs do not mind if parts of the dissertation are published. It would be a problem if someone had previously published a few articles before the PhD and then tried to turn *those* articles into a dissertation. Some institutions see it as an advantage to publish chapters as articles as this helps to demonstrate that the dissertation actually is "publishable," which is one of the criteria for evaluation.

The bigger problem may be that a publisher may not be interested in publishing the dissertation as a monograph if too much of it has already been put into journals. It may be worth talking this over with your supervisor and strategically publishing only a couple of articles out of your dissertation chapters. Also, some monograph series would be concerned if you have already published the "big idea" or main argument of the dissertation in the form of a journal article. Thus, it may be safer to publish exegetical insights or methodological matters that are only ancillary to your main work.

Will I limit myself if I publish with a confessional or denominational journal? There is no need to steer completely clear of confessional or denominational journals. It is true that some potential employers may frown upon such research activity, but you can be selective as far as what you put on your CV. More importantly, strive to publish at least *some* articles in the "world class" category. In the end, part of your academic world is getting your research into the hands of others, and you can best decide which venues you wish to use for this. Also, some topics, such as theological and hermeneutical discussions that relate to ministry or spiritual formation, may be more "at home" in confessional journals.

Can I exceed the suggested word limit for a journal article? A suggested word limit is usually general and offers the potential contributor a sense of what the journal can handle in terms of length. If the suggestion is six to eight thousand words, going over by a few hundred words is probably not a problem. It is a different thing to exceed it by *thousands*. If you are more than 750 words over the limit, I suggest contacting the editor for consultation.

When can you submit another article to the same journal after getting rejected? There are plenty of good journals that fit a wide range of subjects, so you really wouldn't need to send another article to the same journal immediately. I suggest allowing a distance of at least one year before revisiting the same journal for consideration after a rejection.

Can I check in with the editor and find out the status of my article? When? Again, when you send the original email submitting the article to the editor, make sure that you politely request an idea of the time it takes for assessment. Patiently wait until that time has passed before making an inquiry. If you still have not received any information two weeks past that time, it is reasonable to contact the editor again and politely ask for an update. In the summer (May-August) and during winter break (December/January), delays are more likely.

9

Teaching Experience

INTRODUCTION

Most PhD programs in biblical studies are focused on making the student a skilled researcher and an expert in a particular area of study. However, many students go on to seek academic employment in colleges and seminaries where teaching courses is the primary task. Thus, those doctoral students who *only* have research experience are often unprepared or underprepared for their first job. In fact, when the time comes to apply and interview for jobs, employers are specifically looking for candidates, not only with a good degree from a well-respected graduate program, but also a solid basis of experience in teaching.

TEACHING DURING THE PHD

The Basics

Some graduate programs place a strong emphasis on teaching and pedagogy, while others offer very few opportunities and resources. Some students shy away from accepting or pursuing teaching opportunities because it is viewed as a distraction from the doctoral coursework or dissertation research. However, given the high expectations that colleges and seminaries have for competent teachers, it is imperative that candidates demonstrate skill and experience in teaching.

In some programs, there are ample opportunities for becoming a teaching assistant (TA).[1] However, the work of a TA can vary considerably from one institution to another, and even from one department to another. It is useful to get whatever teaching experience you can as early as you can. In some cases, this might involve tutoring struggling students, or perhaps grading objective standard exams (e.g., multiple-choice, true/false, short answer, etc.). In other cases, the work of a TA is more involved, perhaps leading a lab session after a plenary lecture where issues are discussed in more depth or the TA reviews the homework assignment.

It is more common in biblical studies for doctoral students to find opportunities to teach courses in languages, as the textbook provides the plan for the course and subjective aspects of grading are minimized. This can provide an excellent context for learning how to speak clearly and effectively, how to pace lectures, how to adjust the level of difficulty throughout the class as needed, and how to encourage struggling students and manage difficult ones. Though it is rather rare, some students will be given the chance to design a course themselves and work through the important matters of the format of the class (lecture and content, group discussions, spacing of exams), assignments, and textbooks. While this experience can be time-consuming, it does introduce the student to the challenges of teaching and forces him or her to think through models of instruction, course management, and styles of learning and communication.

Finding Teaching Opportunities

If the doctoral program does not provide each student with opportunities for teaching experience, there are other paths that can be pursued. If there are no official TA positions in your program, you might consider asking a professor if you could be an unofficial TA for a course, aiding students who need help and "learning the ropes" of teaching and course development. This will probably not yield much practical experience, but it can be a nice entry into the world of teaching.

Another route is to find a local Bible college or community college nearby where you might inquire about opportunities to teach as an adjunct instructor. In such cases, you might have to teach a course outside of your

1. Some institutions use the language of "preceptor."

specialty or areas of interest (to meet the needs of that institution), but the benefit will be that you will have full charge of the course and how it is designed.

Thirdly, you may consider contacting your former institutions of study and try to teach a summer course. In the summer, you might find an intensive (one-to-three-week course) that would enable you to gain teaching experience while being away only a few weeks. The same could potentially be done if you could find courses that need to be taught in a short "January term." This kind of experience also helps to connect you to another institution and to build contacts.

Finally, many institutions offer online courses that do not require the students or the professor to be in one particular place at one particular time ("asynchronous"). It may be worthwhile to contact some institutions that you may have some connection with (e.g., former institution, friends who teach there, your denominational seminary, etc.) and inquire about potential online teaching opportunities.

If all else fails, you may have to look for teaching opportunities in other settings or in other areas of study. Can you teach ESL (English as a Second Language) courses at a local community center? Is there a way to teach a New Testament or Old Testament survey course at a local church? Are you able to teach Latin or Greek for a homeschooling network? Is there a Christian private high school in your area that needs a part-time religion or Bible teacher? Again, any experience is better than no experience. At job interviews, it is not uncommon to be asked about your teaching philosophy or certain kinds of classroom situations. *How do you handle occasions of conflict with students in the classroom? What is your favorite part of teaching? What is your least favorite?* On such occasions, you do not want to be stuck with the answer, "I have never done any teaching, so I don't know." Even if you have to draw on nonacademic teaching contexts, it shows some reflection on the process and real experience with normal issues that occur in instruction and student-teacher interaction.

ADVICE ON LEARNING TO TEACH

As a Teaching Assistant

As a teaching assistant, your role depends on the needs of the course and the needs of the main instructor. Sometimes it is heavily involved, and may even include giving a lecture. Other times, it is an opportunity to lighten the professor's burden by doing some grading. If you feel a bit unsatisfied with the level of engagement, you may want to talk this over with the professor and politely inquire into how to gain more practical experience. Also, you may want to use the opportunity of being a TA to ask some useful questions from the professor about the course: *Why did you choose the textbook(s) and assignments that you did? What do you hope the students will learn from the course? Why did you arrange the lectures as you did?* If you will not be doing any speaking in class or lecturing, you might ask the professor if you could lead an optional review session for the course before the final exam (perhaps in an evening time that works for the students). This would afford you a chance to practice teaching and interaction.

Teaching Philosophy

When I began teaching full-time, I made a common mistake—I assumed that the best method of teaching was the way that I learned in my own previous educational experience. I sat through three-hour lectures in grad school, so I lectured for three hours when I became a professor. I assigned "exegesis papers" because I had written them. Now, there is nothing wrong with long lectures or exegesis papers *per se.* The point I want to make is that I had not thought through a *teaching philosophy.* I started with books, topics, and assignments, and I assumed good results would come. But it obviously makes more sense to begin with the program, course objectives (and learning outcomes), *and* a teaching philosophy. And then the material flows from these.

But where do you get a teaching philosophy from? There are some online resources that can help you get your bearings straight.[2] But it is important that your teaching philosophy comes from *your* personality, passions, student and institutional culture, and discipline material. Nevertheless, some basics are applicable across the board in higher education. Below is my own approach to teaching.

2. See https://cft.vanderbilt.edu/guides-sub-pages/teaching-statements/.

The Learning Process.

How do you want your students to learn? My personal take is this: establish, engage, and create.

- Establish—that is, the teacher (me) presents key information to the students to give them a foundation in the course material (e.g., history, methodology, concepts).

- Engage—this involves facilitating active and penetrating interaction with the material (e.g., reflections, discussion, field trips).

- Create—this can be any work that requires students to create something related to the content. Often "creating" involves research papers, but depending on student and program needs, it could be any assignment or project that requires fresh thought. Thinking through the learning process in this way has helped me to conceive of how to get students to a place of transformation in their educational experience.

Best Practices.[3] *Below are seven practices that support a good teaching philosophy.*

1) Promote co-learning. Yes, it is helpful for the teacher to give information to students, but it is crucial for students to develop a community of co-learning where they engage with one another. Usually, I establish groups of four to five students in a course, and these become their "discussion groups." A variety of prompts and assignments help to create bonds of trust and co-learning in these groups.

2) Follow the "twenty-minute" rule. Somewhere along the way I picked up on this concept: every twenty minutes of class, try to change up the activity, whether it is having a break, transitioning to discussion, watching a video, or opening it up for questions (etc.). This breaks up monotony, keeps students' attention, and promotes processing through different types of learning and engagement.

3) Think beyond research papers. Now, for some courses, research papers are probably still the best way for students to learn. But otherwise, I

---

3. See http://teachingcenter.wustl.edu/resources/teaching-methods/lectures/tips-for -teaching-with-lectures/ and http://teachingcenter.wustl.edu/resources/course-design/ tips-for-faculty-teaching-for-the-first-time/.

encourage you to find media that are the most relevant to the course material and the lives of the students.

4) Choose depth over breadth of content. When I first started teaching, I felt a mysterious compulsion to pack as much information and reading into a course as possible. But there are important reasons *not* to do this. First, because students nowadays have access to so many good reference works and online material, it is not as pressing that a single course "deliver" so much information. Secondly—and more importantly—students retain information and move towards transformation when space and intentionality are invested in processing presented knowledge more deeply and holistically.

5) Ditch PowerPoint. Again, when I first started teaching, I always used PowerPoint slides. I would cram small text into slides and click through slide after slide of information, with students either feverishly writing each word or (worse) tuning me out because they knew they had access to the slides. I am now realizing that this is not a very effective use of classroom time. More and more I am going "old school," so to speak, and focusing classroom time on discussion.[4] Current conventional wisdom in education promotes two things (in addition to ditching PowerPoint): (1) flip the classroom—deliver information through video lectures and books/readings *outside* of class, so face-to-face time can be more engaging; and (2) keep visuals minimal and unique; that is, feel free to use slides to draw attention to a chart or image of relevance. Use visuals to inspire the imagination, and to communicate in ways that words cannot.

6) Teach civility. If there is one trend I have seen develop rapidly in American culture over the last ten years, it is the unfortunate tendency for students to recede into their ideological echo chambers and reject and judge others who have divergent views. While social media has brought many benefits in education and leisure, it has also created pathways for us to separate ourselves into interest groups full of people who think only like us. It is imperative that higher education students practice listening, civil engagement, and communicating disagreement in productive ways.

7) Make the class interesting, enjoyable, and fun. I wish this would go without saying, but all too often we assume that serious learning has

4. See the scathing article about PowerPoint: Sørensen, "Let's Ban PowerPoint."

to be serious. But what I have come to learn by experience as a teacher is that students often remember and are most impacted by interesting and enjoyable experiences—learning exercises that go beyond transfer of knowledge and touch heart, body, and funny bone. Not all subjects can be "fun," but even a difficult class can be deeply rewarding when the classroom culture is energetic and exciting.

Teaching Greek or Hebrew Grammar

It is quite often the case, as mentioned above, that opportunities arise for graduate students to teach language courses—for biblical studies, Greek and Hebrew. Sometimes you will need to use the textbook that the institution typically uses, and other times it is more flexible. When it comes to choosing a textbook, carefully consider the level of the students and the timeframe involved. Be wary of choosing a textbook just because that was the one that *you* learned from.

If you have any control over the scheduling, it is always advisable, for the purposes of language learning, to meet several times a week for a short period, rather than once a week for a long block of time. For example, if you have three hours a week for class, it is preferable to meet two or three times a week (for one or one-and-a-half hours each session) than to have a three-hour block. Students will be able to handle the material more easily if vocabulary and paradigm memorization are digested in smaller portions throughout the week.

Also, a traditional lecture-style course is not recommended for language learning. With the use of a good, clear textbook, in-class time can best be utilized by providing clarifications, supplementary instruction, and especially by dedicating time to reviewing homework exercises and having "lab" sessions. One suggestion that is often given regarding language instruction is to vary the kinds of learning that take place through the course. One rather perfunctory avenue is textbook reading and visual instruction. However useful and necessary this is, the more types of input that are given to the student, the more likely the material is to "stick." Some teachers have found success in utilizing musical resources where the alphabet, grammar rules, and/or paradigms are sung. Others have tried playing "games" that involve Greek or Hebrew. On a more basic level, instructors could try using real objects as visual aids for learning the foreign language.[5]

Another important tool for learning involves constant student interaction with the language and consistent feedback. That probably means having regular graded homework and spending time in class reviewing the homework. Also, to aid student learning, I recommend supplying students with an answer key to assignments to compare their own translations and answers with that of the textbook author or another professional.[6]

There has been some discussion in recent years regarding the various benefits and drawbacks of teaching students how to use original language Bible software (such as Accordance or Logos).[7] On the one hand, many students who study the biblical languages in graduate school find it difficult to work efficiently and quickly with the Greek or Hebrew text for the benefit of academic study or pastoral ministry (i.e., preaching preparation). Learning how to use software programs could encourage such students to maintain an active use of their grammatical knowledge. On the other hand, it is entirely possible that graduate training in language software could become a crutch and communicate (however wrongly) to the student that facility with the software is a sufficient replacement for critical knowledge of paradigms, syntactical relationships, and a significant aggregate of vocabulary words. One way to limit this latter problem would be to introduce software training only in the last couple of weeks of the course, rather than integrating the training from the start. That way, students are taught the basics of grammar and syntax without relying on the software, but such

5. For example, if you are teaching the students the Greek or Hebrew word for "water," you might bring in a glass of water and point to it every time you say the word "water."

6. This may raise concern over students cheating on their homework by simply using the answer key. There are a few ways around this problem. One solution is to assign all of the exercises, but provide an answer key for the even-numbered questions/exercises. Then, the instructor could grade only the odd-numbered ones (or vice versa). A second solution is to make homework mandatory, but the final grade highly dependent on quizzes and tests. Thus, a student cheating on the homework will only end up having a very minimal effect on the course grade.

7. Many sophisticated biblical language software programs are very expensive. Though they offer optimal functionality for researchers, there are some cheap or free options. In the first year of Greek study, I introduce students to "StepBible," a free program that allows students to do Greek word searches in both the New Testament and the LXX; see https://www.stepbible.org/.

resources are still introduced to provide a significant foundation for efficiently using language knowledge in the future.

Teaching Exegesis Courses

Many students who earn PhDs in biblical studies and go on to teach end up teaching biblical exegesis at some point. In such courses, as you may already know well, a specific biblical book or book set (such as "the Pentateuch" or "Ephesians and Colossians") is studied in depth, often in the original language(s). The intended objectives and purposes of such courses will inevitably vary from one institution and department to another (especially regarding interests in theology, historical criticism, pastoral ministry, history of interpretation, etc.), but we can offer here some general comments.

At the very least, a standard exegesis course should aim at covering at least these three areas: genre, content, and method. In the first place, most students will not have the opportunity to study all of the biblical books (or even an entire corpus such as the Old Testament/Hebrew Bible or the New Testament). Thus, it is important that an exegesis course on a specific book inform students in such as way as to give pointers on how to study the wider genre.[8] Thus, some time should be spent, especially early on in the course, discussing genre interpretation and perhaps reading other samples of documents (biblical and/or non-biblical) within the same genre. Secondly, an exegesis course needs to provide students with significant knowledge of the actual content of the biblical book(s), as well as critical issues pertaining to exegetical cruxes. Finally, it is important for such courses to teach exegetical method, demonstrating on the given text(s) what good interpretation looks like and how it can be done in a somewhat organized fashion.[9] This may involve a review of (or introduction to) basic elements of exegesis such as translation theory, word studies, and semantic structure (or discourse) analysis. Furthermore, advanced exegesis courses should treat, as relevant, such advanced elements as interaction with social science, literary and narrative criticism, rhetoric, reader-centered approaches, etc.[10]

8. For example, a study of Joshua can and should demonstrate how to study historical narrative in general, as well as how to study the individual book *per se.*

9. The best basic exegetical primers are Fee, *New Testament Exegesis*; Gorman, *Elements of Biblical Exegesis*; and Stuart, *Old Testament Exegesis.*

10. While these have been mentioned earlier, I again commend to you Green, *Hearing the New Testament*; and Gooder, *Searching for Meaning.*

Additionally, some kinds of institutions and programs will want to add a fourth dimension of theological or pastoral reflection. In such cases, students should be taught how to work from textual research to analyzing the core message of the text, and on to theological analysis and sermon preparation.[11]

Finally, it is very useful to spend time in an exegesis course training students in the area of critical thinking and the development of fresh ideas and hypotheses, especially if the majority of students are interested in pursuing further graduate work. Too many students, even doctoral students, are poorly trained in these areas and do not read sources "actively" and with a critical eye. Rather, information is statically collected, reordered, and compiled for assignments. Instead, students will gain much from filtering texts as they read, testing and challenging secondary sources, and presenting alternative or counter-proposals when current scholarly answers or avenues are limited or flawed.

Developing a Syllabus

There is no manual that states exactly what should be included in a syllabus. Again, each program and department may have its own required elements. It is quite standard, though, to provide some basic information for the course, including: professor's name and contact details, course name and meeting times/days, course description, course objectives, required reading list, assignment list and deadlines, and a basic schedule regarding what information will be dealt with in each week or session. In addition, it is recommended that the syllabus include something like a "community ethos" where certain standards are set forth regarding class etiquette. You may want to address issues such as punctuality, penalties for absence and late assignments, the importance of constructive comments during group time, and a reminder about shutting off cell phones.

Some instructors have become more concerned with student use of laptops in class, especially as students may be prone to cheating or engaging in various kinds of "distracting" activities such as surfing the web or playing solitaire. Thus, some syllabi mention that laptops are not permitted in the

---

11. For theology and exegesis, see Davis and Hays, *Art of Reading Scripture*; Goldingay, *Models for Interpretation of Scripture*; Green, *Seized by Truth*; Gundry and Meadors, *Four Views on Moving Beyond*; Vanhoozer, *Dictionary for Theological Interpretation*; for preaching, see Achtemeier, *Preaching Hard Texts*; Best, *From Text to Sermon*.

classroom. Weighing the advantages and disadvantages is usually, though, going to be up to instructor.

I encourage you also to present clear statements regarding plagiarism. Some institutions use plagiarism-detecting software called Turnitin (www.turnitin.com). Information theft and lack of source attribution are becoming a major issue in higher education. Many students do not know the specific rules or rationales regarding plagiarism, and with access to so much theological and religious content online, students need thorough instruction in this matter. From my decade of experience in higher education instruction, I have learned that it is much less work to spend time on prevention than on dealing with it after the fact.[12]

Dealing with Student Problems and Conflict

Conflict with students is unavoidable. Indeed, this tends to be one of the most difficult experiences for professors. What do you do if a student comes to you during class or at your office and complains about a grade? First of all, don't get defensive. Sometimes professors can make a mistake, and the student has the right to bring this to their attention. If the confrontation is in the classroom or in the hallway (or cafeteria), I recommend giving a "cooling period" by setting up a time to meet in your office. Often, when a student has had some time to settle down, the one paper or exam seems less urgent. Secondly, you may want to take the exam or paper from the student so that you can review it carefully and privately before discussing it with them.

If you are new to this kind of situation or are feeling especially uncomfortable (based on the student or the situation), you may want to bring it to the attention of your department chair or your dean. This not only brings another professional into the discussion, but it demonstrates that you showed some forethought in the matter.

While you don't want to merely indulge the student by raising the grade, you will want to review your comments and grading technique on that paper or exam to double check that you have graded the work fairly and consistently. When it comes time to meet with the student, you may want to review his or her progress. If the student has excelled in previous

12. Yale's Center for Teaching and Learning has a useful online explanation of plagiarism for educators and students; see https://ctl.yale.edu/writing/using-sources/understanding-and-avoiding-plagiarism/what-plagiarism.

assignments, you may offer some encouragement and mention that his or her overall grade is not in jeopardy if that is the case. If the student has done poorly on repeated assignments, you may warmly invite him or her to visit your office hours or set up another convenient time for additional help in the future.

In my own technique of grading, especially when the material is more subjective (as with essays), I tend to give students "the benefit of the doubt" in some areas and grade more strictly (to make a point on a weak area for the student) in others. That way, when a student complains that I took off too many points in one area, I can assure them that I make it a point to be somewhat generous in other areas to balance that out. It is important, though, that every student's work is graded consistently when using this model.

Another common problem in the classroom is the overly-talkative or opinionated student who offends other students or simply takes up too much discussion time. If the problem is happening in discussion time, and a group member is annoyed, I have encouraged the annoyed student to politely talk to the other student. This can have mixed results, but it is a helpful learning experience for both students and has the advantage of not shaming the student by being called out (publicly or privately) by the professor. If the problem happens during all-class time, you may need to set up a private meeting with the student. As long as the student isn't berated, most people respond respectfully to the conversation. Make sure they know that their voice is important and valued, and encourage them to foster a learning environment where all voices are encouraged and space is made for more reserved or quiet students to contribute.

Finally, it has become common for students to (anonymously) evaluate the professor and the course at the end of the term. Typically, one can expect to receive a mixture of criticism and praise, based on the matchup of learning styles, personality, expectations, and course difficulty, among other things. One unusually negative or hostile evaluation should not be taken too seriously. The purpose of these evaluations is not necessarily to "grade" the work of the professor, but rather to improve the teaching of the course and identify areas of growth for that particular instructor. When all the evaluations are collated, one can see patterns, especially when there are areas where the professor was weak on a consistent basis, whether it involves communicating course expectations, progressing through the material of the course in an appropriate fashion, or demonstrating availability outside the classroom. Again, the key is looking to the future when reading the evaluations and not dwelling on the past.

Avoid the temptation to throw away the evaluations immediately after receiving the results. Keeping a record of evaluations is useful for several reasons. First, you may want to chart how students evaluate the course (both content and pedagogy) over a period of several semesters. Secondly, if you are going to be applying for jobs in the future, sometimes employers ask for a sample of student evaluations to get a sense for the effectiveness of the professor and whether or not he or she is a good communicator and educator.

ADDITIONAL RESOURCES

There plenty of general guides to teaching in higher education, and one can be overwhelmed by this selection. Two of the best, without doubt, are Ken Bain's *What the Best College Teachers Do* and Peter Filene's *The Joy of Teaching*. Aiming at helping new instructors in a wide range of disciplines, these books offer theoretical as well as practical advice regarding best practices and the appropriate ways to perceive the teaching task.

More relevant to biblical studies, the Society of Biblical Literature has developed two texts that address this field more directly: *Teaching the Bible: Practical Strategies for Classroom Instruction* (edited by Mark Roncace and Patrick Gray) and *Teaching the Bible through Popular Culture and the Arts* (also edited by Roncace and Gray). E. Randolph Richards and Joseph R. Dodson have written a handy little text called *A Little Book for New Bible Scholars*, which offers many insights from seasoned teachers. Finally, I highly encourage you to read Gary Burge's *Mapping Your Academic Career: Charting the Course of a Professor's Life*. This book is a goldmine of insight into the stages of professional life in the academy.

On the internet, a host of resources on teaching and learning in religion and theology can be found through the website of the Wabash Center. Advice and resources are provided concerning pedagogical theory, assessment and evaluation, strategies and techniques, special topics (e.g., faith in the classroom, dealing with emotionally intense issues, teaching current events, etc.), professional and personal development, and the use of technology.[13]

---

13. See https://www.wabashcenter.wabash.edu/resources/scholarship-on-teaching/.

The SBL offers a collection of members' syllabi covering these categories: Bible and Religion Introductions, Early Judaism, Hebrew Bible/Old Testament, Intertestamental Texts, Issues in Religion and Biblical Interpretation, Language and Translation, Mediterranean Societies in Biblical Times, New Testament, and The Social World of Ancient Israel.[14] The American Academy of Religion also offers, on its website, an archive of real syllabi submitted by professors. For Biblical studies, you can select the categories "Bible," "Bible—Hebrew Bible/Old Testament," or "Christian Origins."[15]

The internet has made it possible for those who teach biblical studies to learn from one another and come together as instructors. Since much of a professor's work is teaching (alongside some research and administration), it is beneficial to spend time thinking about teaching and learning strategies and how to make courses more interesting and effective.

14. https://www.sbl-site.org/publications/article.aspx?ArticleId=673.
15. See https://www.aarweb.org/programs-services/syllabus-project.

10

Job Hunting, Interviewing, and Publishing the Dissertation

THE JOB HUNT

Introduction

Getting into a good PhD program, as you may well know, is only half the battle for those seeking a life in the academy. Also, it is not enough to pursue the PhD and put off thinking about the job hunt until the dissertation is over. Like anything else, the more thought you can invest in understanding the road ahead, the better prepared you will be. For example, there are many different kinds of institutions, and knowing in advance which kind you want to be most prepared for can afford you the opportunities to seek out experience that will be especially meaningful for that kind of position. For biblical studies, we might break institution types down into three basic kinds. First we have the small liberal arts college (confessional or not). In such schools, the focus is on providing a solid education for students. This is accomplished through a heavy investment on the faculty's end on availability to students, modest class sizes, and a strong commitment to excellent teaching. Students tend to prefer such a school due to its size and the distinctive character, personality, and reputation of the institution.

The second kind of institution is the public university, which often tends to be a research university. While teaching is certainly important at such places, high demands are placed on the faculty in the area of innovation and new research. Some are attracted to the large size of the public university, which has enough of an endowment and tuition money to maintain state-of-the-art facilities, outstanding libraries, and attract the finest faculty. One potentially advantageous feature of the public university is the possibility of teaching at both the graduate and undergraduate levels. Many small liberal arts schools do not have graduate programs, and freestanding seminaries do not offer undergraduate courses.

The third major category is seminaries—that place where students study at a graduate level for the purpose of training pastors, missionaries, various Christian workers, and of course future scholars of religion, theology, and biblical studies. Many people who pursue a PhD in biblical studies attended seminary at some point and, thus, are interested in finding a position at one.

When it comes to being prepared for such institutions, some kinds of experiences are universally important, such as administrative experience. However, each kind of institution will be looking for specific sorts of things. For example, the liberal arts college will probably be more interested in the candidate's teaching experience and public communication skills than their future research plans. The research university, alternatively, may not only be interested in the candidate's research capabilities and potential, but also may look for any experience in the area of supervising student research.[1] A seminary may be interested in teaching experience particularly at the master's or graduate level.[2] When it comes to job applications, it is normal for candidates to apply for a wide range of positions, but knowing your own strengths and making specific preparations regarding one or two types can provide an edge over other candidates.

1. While it is unusual for a doctoral student or recent graduate to have supervised PhD students, it may be possible to get experience supervising master's students. Or, in the United Kingdom in particular, it is possible to supervise an undergraduate research project. If all else fails, you may consider asking your supervisor or another professor if you could sit in on some supervisory sessions that he or she has with a master's student and learn about the process and good mentorship.

2. A seminary or Christian college may also be looking for evidence of experience in ministry, such as pastoral work or active participation as an elder or committee member in the local church. Some seminaries may request a reference, alongside regular academic ones, from your pastor or priest that focuses on church commitment.

Finding Jobs

Today, the internet is the primary place where one can find academic job postings for biblical studies. However, it is probably not going to be a good use of time to check general employment websites like www.monster.com or www.careerbuilder.com. There are a few websites where colleges, universities, and seminaries tend to advertise when the position is in the area of religion or, more specifically, biblical studies.

1. https://www.aarsbl.org/. Most departments of religion and/or theology are aware of the Society of Biblical Literature and will post jobs through their employment services (in conjunction with the American Academy of Religion). This is, perhaps, the best place to look for jobs specifically in Old Testament or New Testament, but you should be aware that only paying society members have access to this site.

2. www.higheredjobs.com/faculty. While this website is not as narrowly focused as AAR/SBL, it offers a steady stream of job advertisements from research universities to community colleges.

3. https://www.cccu.org/career-center/. Under the auspices of the Council for Christian Colleges & Universities, you can find jobs at Christian liberal arts schools.

4. www.jobs.ac.uk. This website serves academic institutions in the United Kingdom.

The Application Process

Cover Letter

Much like PhD applications, for jobs the process generally starts quite early. For example, for a position that begins in the fall of 2019, the advertising post might come as early as the summer of 2018 (over a year in advance). For biblical studies in particular, there is a general push for search committees to post the job early enough that interviews can be set up for the SBL annual meeting in November (of the year prior to the beginning of the academic year for the job). The period between the initial advertising of the post and the deadline when applications have to be received ranges between three and nine months in general. It is usually no less than three months because it takes applicants time to acquire references, write cover letters, and provide additional information, such as sample syllabi and student course evaluations.

Generally, academic applications consist of three fixed features: cover letters, references, and the CV. The cover letter serves a variety of purposes. It "covers" the applicant (name and contact info), the particular position, and the applicant's general interest in that job and institution and his or her suitability as a qualified candidate.

Perhaps the most critical (and most common) mistake that potential job candidates make is that they do not tailor their cover letters to relate specifically to each institution of application. Instead, many people write a generic cover letter and send it off to multiple schools. However, beyond basic academic criteria and expectations, most hiring schools are interested in "institutional fit"—*does the candidate fit well into the background, ethos, and mission statement of the school?* It is imperative, then, that the issue of "institutional fit" factors into the cover letter. This will require you to do some homework on the background of the school and what makes it tick. To gain further insight into the inner workings of the school, you may want to contact someone you know that teaches there, or a current or former student.

If the school is confessional, you will want to pay close attention to the school's statement of faith and general theological persuasions. If it is a denominational seminary or college, you may want to mention your commitment to that tradition and any professional experience (e.g., pastoral internships, ordination, etc.).[3]

---

3. Certainly an institution's website is going to supply a vast amount of information about that school. Get a sense for the places where the faculty (in your field) studied, the makeup of students and their backgrounds, the number of students, and where the faculty stands theologically (if appropriate). You may also want to look at who was hired there most recently, what institutions they came from, and where they studied. Much information about the atmosphere at the school can be gleaned from looking at past issues of the student magazine or newspaper. If you want to get a better sense of the academic interests of the department, search the SBL website for the last three to five years of the annual meeting with the search criteria of the institution's name—you will not only see which faculty members are actively presenting (and their subjects of interest), but you may also see what students are doing and what kind of "presence" that institution has in biblical studies.

Curriculum Vitae

It is not necessary here to rehearse the elements of a CV, as the basic items will remain essentially the same as for the PhD application (see chapter 3). Perhaps the three most important categories of the job-seeking CV are (1) education, (2) teaching experience, and (3) publishing record. Thus, these areas should be front-and-center on the CV. Hiring schools are especially concerned that the candidate either *already has obtained the PhD* or *will be completing the PhD soon*. If you have not yet completed the PhD and you are in the last stages (especially in the last year), you may want to write down on the CV your expected submission date.

The length of an academic CV is considerably more different than for other fields of employment. Given the importance of publications in particular, a long CV is quite tolerable. However, that does not mean that one should throw in everything imaginable (e.g., leave out hobbies, marital status, children's names, etc.). I would suggest having a CV that is no longer than six pages of essential information. Also, one easy way that many schools dispense with applications is to throw out those that include CVs with spelling and grammar errors. Thus, you will want to proofread all of your application materials thoroughly and, if possible, have another colleague or professional have a look at it as well.

References

In general, hiring institutions request three recommendations from academic professionals for the application. If you are a relatively recent PhD graduate (or a current student), it is expected that your supervisor will serve as one referee. How do you choose other referees? The most suitable referees tend to be other professors within the doctoral program with whom you took courses, or professors from previous institutions. It is important, though, to keep in mind the matter of "institutional fit"—think through whether you know anyone that can serve as a suitable referee that has friends at the institution of interest or is well-respected by that school.

For the job-hunting season (which tends to be from August to December especially), you may want to politely give potential referees some notice that you will probably need several references over the next several months. For each application, make a request for a reference (on email with updated CV attached) well in advance of the deadline, preferably more than a month. I also tend to follow up with the referee again about a week before the deadline in the off-chance that he or she forgot.

Additional Items in the Application Packet

Sometimes it may be possible that information is requested for the application beyond the cover letter, CV, and references. Some schools ask for a statement of teaching or teaching philosophy. In such a case, the format and content can vary quite widely from one discipline to the next, and even from one person to the next. The purpose of such a document is to articulate your teaching method(s), approaches, expertise, and attitudes. You will want to answer questions like: *Why do you want to teach as a career? How do you go about facilitating the learning process? Why do you believe your manner of teaching is effective or useful?* The search committee is probably not looking for any particular answer, but will want to know that you have consciously thought through the way you teach. There is, thus, no need to make this a lengthy document, but such a statement can be made in less than six hundred words.

Some confessional schools (and especially seminaries) may require you to answer questions about your theological positions or to write a statement of faith. Here, they want to ensure that you are on the same page in terms of theological commitments. That does not necessarily mean that the institution does not value diversity in thought. Rather, before they move forward with candidates, they want to be able to eliminate those applicants that clearly do not align with the theological positions of the school.

Once in a while, an institution may request a writing sample. In such a case, it is best to supply something published, like a journal article. If you have not published an article, you may supply a lengthy published review or, if necessary, a portion of the dissertation.

You want to be careful not to include too many things in the application, especially if they are not asked for. An oppressively thick application file can come across as desperate and can sometimes seem like more work than it is worth.

First-Round Interviews

Hiring institutions in biblical studies (especially in America) tend to go through two rounds of interviews. The first round tends to be either on the phone (or Skype) or, more commonly, at a conference such as the SBL annual meeting in November. From the dozens of applicants, the search committee usually narrows it down to eight to ten top candidates that are invited for an interview. At conference interviews, because the timetable is accelerated with so many candidates being interviewed during one week-end or only a few days, your own session with the committee members may be only twenty to forty-five minutes. In preparation for this interview, ask whoever contacted you about the interview to inform you about the names of the committee members that will be interviewing you. Learn as much as you can about each of those people prior to the interview—you may have some common interest or background that you can mention.

During the interview, arrive on time (if not slightly early) and dress professionally. Typically an interview will start casually, where you are asked general questions about yourself and your background. Stick closely to your academic life and background (not hobbies or family life) and keep answers brief. After the initial set of general questions, the rest of the time will be spent getting to know you as a professional. Liberal arts colleges will be asking questions about teaching experience, methods, textbooks, conflict resolution techniques, subject interests, range of teaching, leader-ship experiences, etc. Research-driven schools may ask you to summarize your dissertation, as well as plans for future research. Again, keep your statements concise and to-the-point. Wherever possible, explain how your interests intersect with other faculty members. Also, make it clear that you know how that school works. Don't ask questions about school size or who teaches in that department. You should already know the answer to these questions. Instead, ask questions you can't get the answers from elsewhere: *Why has this position opened? What are the strengths of the department? What kinds of courses need to be filled?*

It is too early at the first interview to ask about salary, health benefits, moving details, etc. This can wait for a second round situation. Rather, you want to spend this first interview making a good impression as a competent professional who seems easy to work with and right for the institution.

In terms of attitude and rapport, the more calm and comfortable you feel and come across in the interview the better. Be aware of nervous habits (tapping your feet, biting your nails, sweating excessively) and de-fensive answers—take ostensibly loaded or pointed questions in the best light possible.[4] A small amount of (appropriate) humor can go a long way to show that you are a "normal" person that can carry on an enjoyable conversation.

Even if you are still a PhD student at this stage, walk into the interview not as a lower member of academic society, but as a potential colleague of your interviewers. At the end of the interview, it is appropriate to ask when you will receive more information regarding the remainder of the search process if the interviewers have not already done so.

Second-Round or Campus Interviews

Often, schools will further narrow the search down to finalist candidates that will be invited to campus for a more thorough interview and to allow them to become more acquainted with the school, faculty, facilities, and atmosphere. For purposes of feasibility, it is rare to have more than five candidates invited to campus (as the school usually foots the bill for airfare and personal expenses, and it takes a great amount of time for the committee to meet with the candidates and make a final recommendation to the administration).

Following the SBL annual meeting timetable, campus interviews usually follow in the months of December through February (about one to three months after the first interview). Some schools will require more time to work through the process, while other schools are anxious to make a selection and complete the process.

If you are interested in pursuing the position and the invitation is extended, I suggest you prepare yourself well for going to campus. Download the current academic catalog (to get to know the curriculum, policies, history, and faculty better) and read any other literature available, such as departmental advertisements, or a copy of the institution's journal if available. This is also a good time to prepare some answers about teaching. For instance, it is not uncommon to be asked questions about the kinds of courses that need to be taught through the open position at the school. If you are told what courses in particular need to be filled, you can begin to think through textbooks, assignments, and how you would structure lecture time and group discussions.

---

4. Once an interviewer asked me if my variety in subject matter in my published articles is a sign of being a "dilettante." While this came across as rude, I tried to explain how I sought to have well-rounded knowledge and interests.

In terms of professional etiquette, knowing that the school will pay for expenses, try to be conservative and thrifty wherever possible. Your spending at this stage may be a positive or negative reflection on your attitude towards money and departmental resources as a colleague. In cooperation with the department chair or dean, book the travel arrangements and accommodations as soon as you can to ensure the best price. While traveling, don't starve yourself to save money, but don't go for the steak dinner every meal.

The actual experience of the campus interview will vary from one school to the next. One should expect, especially in America, that it will involve at least one full day, if not two to three. This time is spent carrying out four purposes. First, the search committee will continue to get to know the candidate and gauge their suitability as a member of the faculty. Second, the candidate will meet with various members of the administration, such as the dean of the college or a provost, to further probe the question of "institutional fit." Thirdly, the candidate is given an opportunity to learn more about the school through tours, meetings with human resources, and perhaps even a look around in the general area (to get a sense for the locale and the flavor of the surroundings). Finally, the candidate is usually required to either offer a lecture to a group of students or to present a piece of research to faculty (and sometimes also graduate students). This last part, in fact, is quite important, and can be the make-or-break portion of the campus visit. My advice for the teaching time is to do more than "lecture." This is an opportunity to put into practice your teaching philosophy and showcase your teaching skills. Be sure to focus on the level of the audience (freshmen, senior seminar, first year of seminary, etc.) and provide an interesting and informative session that mixes teaching and at least some discussion.

Don't expect to be grilled constantly during the campus visit. At this stage, you have proven yourself to be someone that they want to get to know better and on whom they want to make a good impression.

Due to the fact that the interview process is extended over a couple of days, it is difficult to always be "on." However, you must continue to treat every conversation (even with the student who picked you up at the airport) as part of the whole package of the interview. An off-color or inappropriate statement could come back to haunt you.

In terms of interview questions, you will probably be asked similar ones to those from an earlier interview, but now with more detail and wider audiences. The topic of teaching will probably be the main focus at many schools. Though it is cliché, it is important that you be yourself and that you don't try to fit some kind of fake persona that you presume the committee wants to see. Your CV will probably give you away anyway. However, there are some key ideas and concepts that are valued by institutions across the board, and you would do well to invest some time in thinking about them.

First, when it comes to teaching, educators are especially impressed by professors who are *creative*—who engage in various styles of teaching and learning and who develop unique assignments. Secondly, there is a growing interest in teaching the Bible using cultural tools and the arts. For example, you might discuss teaching a course on the New Testament, in part, by discussing how it has influenced the visual arts (such as paintings from the Renaissance or in film). Thirdly, studies have shown that students thrive on interdisciplinary studies—where a course can integrate more than one field. How can you demonstrate a facility in interdisciplinarity? Finally, particularly attractive are those educators who are proactive in using technology in the classroom. Not just creating PowerPoint slides, but utilizing new web resources, e-learning platforms, and (perhaps specifically for biblical studies) the integration of the teaching of Bible software programs.

To best prepare and navigate through the process, it may help to know how a search committee works.[5] When a faculty search is approved by the administration, a committee is formed of about three to five faculty members, with one member serving as chair. While several of the members will inevitably be from the department that is hiring, some members may come from other departments or subfields. Often these professors are dealing with the search responsibilities amidst an already-busy teaching and research burden. Ultimately, they deliberate and make a recommendation to an executive officer (such as the dean). This executive officer, taking into account the notes and counsel of the committee, makes the final decision, or presents a decision to a provost, president, and/or board of trustees.

If I have seen one common mistake made by candidates, it is poor preparation for interviews. Once you have been offered an interview, make sure you do as much work as you can to familiarize yourself with the institution and the faculty of the department. If you come across as unaware of basic information (background of the school, faculty members, location, denomination, etc.), it appears that you have too little invested in the interview.

5. For an insider discussion of the process of a search, see Lou Marinoff's essay in *Insidehighered.com* here: http://www.insidehighered.com/advice/2009/08/31/marinoff.

PUBLISHING YOUR DISSERTATION AS A MONOGRAPH

While not universal, most doctoral students in biblical studies intend to publish their dissertation as an academic book, usually in a respected monograph series. For New Testament, some of the most well-respected series are:

- Beihefte zur Zeitschrift für die neutestamentliche Wissenschaft und die Kunde der älteren Kirche
- Biblical Interpretation Series
- Library of New Testament Studies
- Novum Testamentum Supplement Series
- Society of Biblical Literature Monograph Series
- Society of New Testament Studies Monograph Series
- Wissenschaftliche Untersuchungen zum Neuen Testament II.[6]

How does one choose a series with which to publish? There is, of course, the issue of prestige—does the publisher have a reputation for producing eminent volumes in your field? You will also need to consider "fit"—Would that series fit your topic well? After that, there are a host of other considerations.

1. Does the series require a certain maximum word count? If your dissertation is a hundred thousand words, and the series has a limit of eighty thousand words, some authors find the task of editing and condensing the work to be undesirable. Others, however, consider it an advantage to have the opportunity to rework the dissertation to improve the argumentation and eliminate extraneous material.

2. Does the publisher bear the burden of typesetting the manuscript for publication? When a manuscript is published as a book, the text must be typeset—that is, formatted appropriately. The text needs to be "set" into the layout, font, and style of the series. For most trade publications, the publisher is responsible for typesetting the text. However,

---

6. For Old Testament studies, one could publish with the SBL Monograph Series or the Biblical Interpretation Series, as listed here. In additional, one might consider the Beihefte zur Zeitschrift für die alttestamentliche Wissenschaft, the Forschungen zum Alten Testament I, the Library of Hebrew Bible/Old Testament Studies, the Society for Old Testament Study Series, and the Supplements to Vetus Testamentum.

with monograph series and other academic publications, often the author is given this duty or must pay a fee for the publisher to carry out this task. This can be very time-consuming and/or expensive. It is worthy of consideration in the decision.

3. Does the publisher normally accept the manuscript (if it is based on a dissertation) "as is," or are significant adjustments and modifications typically required? Some series desire to keep the monographs as close to the defended dissertations as possible, while others wish to develop and refine the works further.

4. Is the publisher proactive in marketing books? This factor is important, not only in terms of sales, but also when it comes to getting the book out there for journals to review. As a book is bought and frequently reviewed, then the author feels more satisfied that the reading public is aware of it and it is sufficiently available to them. So, another important related question to ask is this: do I see the books in this series regularly reviewed in leading academic journals?

5. What is the general price range of books published in the series? It is common among most monograph series to have relatively high prices (sometimes well over a hundred dollars). Part of the reason is that monographs go through short print runs since they don't tend to be purchased by individuals, but rather libraries and institutions.

6. What kinds of "perks" are provided by the publisher? Authors who publish in some monograph series tend not to receive royalty payments. However, it is customary to receive a complimentary set of copies of the monograph (often between five and twenty).

7. What is the rate of acceptance? How many books are published per year? If you find it a priority to publish the monograph quickly, you may want to investigate the rate of acceptance/rejection for a publisher of interest.

On balance, the most important factor that most authors consider is the issue of series reputation. Beyond that, I would recommend asking mentors, friends, and colleagues about their experiences.[7] Another factor is rapport with the publishing editor and the series editors. Once you

---

7. On my own blog, I conducted a set of interviews with authors that published their dissertations with the top five series for New Testament. See https://cruxsolablog. com/monograph-series/.

make contact (usually via email) with the editors, you will get a feel for their personalities, and it may influence you, one way or the other, about wanting to work with them.

When you have chosen your favorite or first choice, keep in mind that most publishers do not approve of an author sending his or her manuscript to more than one publisher at once. You will need to send it to one publisher at a time, as the review of a proposal is time-consuming and demands much from the hired or requested scholarly assessors.

You will most likely need to send an electronic (and/or hard copy) of the manuscript along with a basic book proposal (whose format and content will usually be laid out on the publisher's website). Generally, the proposal itself will consist of sections such as author information (contact details, background, teaching position), book title, book description (250–500 words), an outline or table of contents, a description of the intended readership (for monographs, it is professional researchers and advanced students), competitive or similar books, the manuscript length, and the expected date of completion (if the author has yet to make final additions/changes).

When the manuscript is basically a modified dissertation, the editor(s) often contact the doctoral examiners (who judged and passed the dissertation) to discuss the book's suitability for publication. Thus, the publisher may ask for the name and contact details of the examiners, and perhaps also the supervisor. The process of assessment varies from one publisher to the next. Receiving the final verdict may take between two to nine months.

Once the offer of publication has been made, how long the process of editing and typesetting takes depends on the changes required and the availability of the author in making those modifications. Often, the changes and typesetting (assuming typesetting falls to the author) can be done in less than a year, if sufficient time is available. Once the typeset manuscript has been submitted back to the publisher, the turnaround time to publication can be very quick, as the hard part (typesetting) has already been done. Many publishers can commit to having the book "in print" within six months of receiving the typeset copy. It is imperative, though, that the author carefully proofreads the manuscript at several stages throughout the process of publishing. That is, inadvertent mistakes can happen through format changes and the necessary modifications of typesetting. Thus, once the whole manuscript is completely reformatted, you should take time to reread the manuscript and identify any errors that remain.

PUBLISHING YOUR SECOND BOOK

In time, most new professors and PhD graduates start to think about their next writing project. The skills that one learns during the research for a dissertation are obviously meant as preparation for future writing. However, there is no need to presume that the next book must be a scholarly monograph. Many educators and scholars write introductory materials, reference works, commentaries, and textbooks.

It is sensible, if you can, to coincide your research with your teaching load, trying to research and write in the areas related to the courses you will be teaching over two or three years. Such a maneuver lends itself to benefiting the teaching itself as well as handling work time more efficiently.

Choosing a publisher for the second book is similar to the first monograph. Prestige is important, though perhaps it will not be the top consideration. If you are looking to get the book into the hands of many scholars and students, you will need to consider how books by various publishers are priced. And, of course, there is the financial dimension, though even the most generous publishers offer very little pay via royalties. You would need to sell tens of thousands of copies of a book to begin to see book publishing as a money-making part of your career!

11

Advancing towards a More Healthy, Diverse, and Inclusive Academy

This chapter has been added to this second edition due to the pressing need for the biblical studies academy to address more directly and thoroughly the problem of discrimination, marginalization, and unfair bias. Whether you are white or not, or male or not, I hope you will read this through to the end. I also hope that women scholars and scholars of color will find helpful guidance, encouragement, and renewed courage and hope.

When I was a teenager, I overheard my father giving advice to my older brother (who was in college, then heading to medical school): "Because you are Indian, because you are different, you are going to have to work harder than everyone else. You have to prove you are the best, or else you will not get any respect." At that time, I thought my dad was exaggerating. *It can't be that bad*, I thought. *Intelligent people don't discriminate. He's being oversensitive.* My ignorance in this persisted for many years. Throughout college, seminary, and doctoral studies, I sustained the presumption that I was not treated unfairly because of my skin color or my name.

In fact, it was only a few years ago that a non-white colleague of mine taught me about "white (male) normalcy" in such a way that transformed my perspective. He emphasized that discrimination often happens below the level of direct intention and consciousness; that is, many people reinforce white normalcy without knowing it. Bias and discrimination pervade, invisibly, and those with the privilege of being white and male almost never see it—unless they are looking for it. I came to realize, looking back, that there were probably occasions where unconscious bias on the part of others had a negative effect on me and my career. Thankfully, I survived graduate studies without much drama or trauma, and I was fortunate to find gainful employment.

Another wakeup call happened when I was interviewing for a job. On the campus visit, I was given a schedule with all the meetings listed. Most of the meetings had clear objectives—human resources, search committee, president, dean, etc. But there was a particular one-on-one faculty meeting that had no topic or goal explicated. When I met with that black female faculty member, it became clear that she was put on my schedule to talk to me about navigating the college life and culture as an ethnic minority. Again, still in my period of ignorance, I initially thought this was overly cautious. But now, almost ten years later, I serve on a faculty-of-color committee at my current institution, and I am keenly aware of how desperately this group's voice and perspectives are needed.

I also want to address the unique challenges that women face in the academy. In 2014, Professor Helen Bond (University of Edinburgh) publicly shared her personal experience.[1] She notes that she was the only woman in her cohort of doctoral students (about twenty-five in all), and she recognized that she was treated differently. While the men would regularly talk research with one another, "to me they'd comment on my hair or my clothes." Bond observes that instances of sexism were often subtle, not ostentatious; she would be called "my dear"—and one scholar introduced her as "Helen Blonde" by accident, but immediately commented, "Well, she is a blonde." She recounts observing another situation where a conference presider gave professional introductions to the male speakers, but had the one female presenter introduce herself. Bond confesses that there is a major

---

1. Bond, "Sexism and NT Leadership." See also the sobering personal account of Dr. Ruth Tucker regarding her experience of sexism and discrimination: Tucker, "12 Year Update."

obstacle to bringing these problems to the attention of her male colleagues: she would be called "prickly" or "oversensitive."

Dr. Lynn Cohick, New Testament scholar and provost at Denver Seminary, has also publicly shared some of the difficulties she has faced as a female in the academy.[2] She recognizes that sometimes she has been asked to contribute to a book or series seemingly as a token female. While she appreciates opportunities to publish, she wonders if her work will be judged differently—*will others simply presume her work is subpar because of her gender?* Cohick states, "I would want a young, male New Testament scholar to look up to me as much as a female New Testament scholar would."

The same concerns that Cohick has about potential "tokenism" I share as a nonwhite scholar. *Will I be taken seriously? Will I be respected and treated fairly regardless of my skin color or heritage?* Marybeth Gasman (University of Pennsylvania) directs the Penn Center for Minority Serving Institutions and has worked hard to advocate for faculty of color. Once, when she was asked why colleges don't hire more ethnic minorities, she gave this frank reply: "We simply don't want them."[3] Often search committees will state that minority candidates don't meet "quality" standards, but Gasman notes that going to an elite school and being mentored by elite scholars is tied up with "social capital and systemic racism." Everyone seems to know the problem—minorities aren't being socially and economically supported through the education process—but no one wants to change this. Gasman also points out that often white scholars will receive subtle benefits; rules will be bent, bridges built, but scholars of color have to "play by the rules." "Let me tell you a secret," Gasman notes, " exceptions are made for white people constantly in the academy; exceptions are the rule in academe." Ultimately, she states, it comes to down to whether or not institutional leaders, administrators, and faculty *actually* believe in the necessity and benefits of diversity and inclusion. For many, it sounds "nice," but it is not treated as a fundamental "need." She encourages educators to reflect on these questions: How many books, articles, or training sessions have you attended on how to recruit faculty of color? How many times have you reached out to departments with great diversity in your field and asked them how they attract and retain a diverse faculty? How often do you resist when someone asks you to bend the rules for faculty of color hires but think it's absolutely

2. Bird, "Lynn Cohick."

3. Gasman, "Ivy League Professor."

necessary when considering a white candidate (you know, so you don't lose such a wonderful candidate)?

EXPERIENCES AND CHALLENGES IN THE ACADEMY

In the summer of 2018, I informally surveyed two dozen female scholars and/or scholars of color (mostly residing in the United States), asking them to answer two questions: What are the unique challenges that women and people of color face in the AAR/SBL academy? What advice or encouragement would you give to those entering this world? We will begin with the challenges and experiences in the academy, and then move on to advice and encouragement.

It's Still a White Man's World

Many scholars have confessed to me that the guild of biblical studies continues to be dominated by white males, and those who do not fit this norm struggle to survive and thrive. One colleague told me, "Women are warmly accepted into the white man's work, while things continue to be done the same way as before." Many women noted that they feel ignored or belittled in their departments and at meetings. Men will often cut them off, talk over them, or simply just ignore their input. Some men may testify that female scholarship is valuable, but the reality is that many institutions still do not take their work seriously. A friend mentioned to me that in her doctoral program she was required to write reviews of thirty-five key works in Old Testament studies—and *none* of them were written by women. For her comps (comprehensive exams), she had to read almost two hundred books, and by her calculation less than 4 percent were by women. The net effect of all of this is that women can feel imposter syndrome rather acutely as they push to find their place in the academy: *Do I really belong here? Will I be happy? How impenetrable is the status ceiling?*

There are many other challenges or obstacles that women face. Doctoral programs are simply not designed with women in mind. For example, few departments have clear and generous policies related to maternity leave. Or accommodations for nursing mothers. There are lots of other challenges that most men do not have to think about—like finding hotels at academic conferences that have refrigerators in the room for breastmilk or baby food. (Not to mention the challenges of *bringing* a baby to an academic meeting!)

For mothers of young children, full-time doctoral studies are brutally dif-ficult. Part-time options are ideal, but few elite programs have such con-siderations in mind. One woman commented that, as a single woman with no children, she found that men did not talk to her, but also that she had trouble relating to married women with families. Another person divulged to me the story of a friend of hers who was assaulted by two fellow stu-dents; and when the incident was reported it was not taken seriously by the institution.

One African-American scholar I spoke with candidly shared that white peers often assumed he was not well educated (even though he had degrees from top schools). Lecturers and fellow students would talk down to him: "I recall professors being genuinely surprised when I turned in well-written and well-reasoned papers." An Asian doctoral student admit-ted that white students sometimes didn't invite him to social gatherings, because they probably assumed he spent time with other Asians. But it seemed that white students were always invited to all kinds of gatherings.

Mentors Wanted

Across the board, almost every single person that I interviewed mentioned the feeling of loneliness and isolation—and the relative lack of available mentors by people *like* them. One woman said that a female mentor would have been beneficial for even small matters "like what to wear to a profes-sional conference, or what to do when a male editor wanted to discuss a book project over a drink in a bar."

For African Americans, there are so few senior scholars in the acad-emy that mentorship can feel impossible. One interviewee told me that he was the first African American to get the PhD from his department. He had no African American mentors at his institution, and he said famous schol-ars elsewhere simply did not have time to spend with him. He felt that a mentor could have helped him to navigate career questions, whereas white colleagues tend to have networks of support to help with these matters.

"Can You Do This for Me?"

Women scholars and people of color confess to having two divergent expe-riences (often at the same time): severe neglect in institutional life (espe-cially leadership), and also being asked to serve on numerous committees and leading diversity training sessions. Studies show that women do more institutional service than men on average. This appears to be in part because women feel that they must demonstrate their productivity, their cooperation, and their "team mentality" in order to justify their positions. Therefore, it is hard to say no; one interviewee wondered, "would I even be *allowed* to say no?" I definitely know this experience. I get asked to write on diversity issues, to serve on diversity committees, and to help with institutional diversity training. Sometimes I am paid for this work, which is nice, but, again, I too wonder if I am allowed to say no. *If I don't do it, will anyone else step up?* The work of being a "diversity" representative is important, and I like to do it when I have the time, but it does take away from research time. *Will that be factored into my tenure review?*

Money Talks

Despite the stories we sometimes tell ourselves about how "fair" and "equal" the academy is, money often shows the true story. One female scholar recounted to me how she got paid less than her male colleagues in her department even though she was at the same or higher rank and more prolific in scholarship. She had to fight for equal wages. An African American scholar mentioned that people of color often do not have networks where they learn about how to best apply for doctoral scholarships and grants. While things sometimes look "fair" on paper, there is a social reality that is clearly skewed.

I Am More than an Ideology

Several scholars mentioned that, on the one hand, they are called upon to represent a certain perspective or value (feminist criticism, African American interpretation, Latina/o interpretation, etc.), but then are treated as if these areas are secondary to "historical criticism"—and it can seem that "historical criticism" is coded language for Eurocentric or white interpretation. The history of African Americans or women in biblical studies and biblical interpretation is treated as supplementary or a "hobby." I remember encountering a new academic study Bible that had supplemental essays written by almost all white, male theologians. The one or two non-white authored essays were on global theology or intercultural ministry, topics that often get assigned to people of color—but then these same scholars are not considered for the "main" essay topics. Several scholars mentioned to me that they don't want to *only* be the "feminist scholarship" female scholar, or the "Latina/o criticism" scholar, but they end up getting attention and opportunities in the guild when they fill these roles.

ADVICE AND ENCOURAGEMENT

Whew. That is a lot to take in. And, to be honest, it has prevented some people from entering the guild, many from thriving, and has even led some to exit academia. There is much to lament in all of this, but I am hopeful. While those I surveyed were very frank with their negative experiences, they all expressed optimism and saw potential for a better future. Below is a summary of their collective advice to women and people of color.

Don't Give Up

This is a crucial message. Many will face an uphill battle to find a home in the academy. The criticism and loneliness can be crushing. But we have seen some space open up for a more diverse and inclusive guild in more recent years. You can't give up on your dreams because the road is long and dangerous. Knowing that there are advocates and friends out there, be courageous. Stand up for yourself, and stand up for others.

Be Yourself

In the fight to "fit in," it is easy to lose yourself—your heritage, your cultural voice, your identity. Be careful not to suppress these things just because institutions often press for assimilation and uniformity. Of course, there are times where differences must be set aside; there are moments when you must hold your tongue (or *not* write that email, text, or tweet). But *never* should anyone be led to feel shame or face rejection because of their gender or the color of their skin. One interviewee offered the important suggestion to find a smaller niche of scholarship and get to know those people. Don't try to struggle to make a big splash across the biblical studies world at large, but invest in a more specialized group at SBL or in another society. Through those relationships hopefully you will find opportunities to present and advance your research, and a place where you can be yourself.

Fight—but Also Forgive

Fight for your rights and for space in order that your voice and perspective can be heard. But there will be many occasions where others trample on your feelings, your heart, your soul, your research, etc. I have witnessed academics hold on to anger, hatred, and bitterness, and the toxicity eats them alive. Forgiveness doesn't mean condoning bad behavior. Use the systems at your disposal to seek fair treatment. But, even if for your own health, it is important to forgive.

Find a Safe Community

The worst thing to do is go it alone. Isolation is often deeply crippling for female scholars and scholars of color. Virtually everyone I have talked to has admitted to the need for an encouraging group of peers and mentors. Sometimes this cannot happen in one's own cohort, department, or institution. So, it might be through a special program,[4] or a more spontaneously formed group that gets together during SBL. Or perhaps a group that has a closed Facebook group where they can share their struggles and offer friendship and support to one another. One female scholar told me that during her doctoral program, many of the women students gathered monthly for lunch and she often left uplifted by kind words and helpful advice. Another female scholar mentioned that she focuses less on attending presentations at conferences and more on networking, because relationships have been so instrumental for her social and emotional health, and also for her professional growth.

Become a Mentor

Last, but not least, several interviewees offered the encouragement that more mentors are needed. It does not necessarily require special skills to be a mentor to female scholars and scholars of color. You don't have to be a certain age, achieve a special status, or have served in academic leadership roles in the past. From my perspective, what is needed is attentiveness

---

4. For example, the Institute for Biblical Research annual ethnic minority breakfast, or women scholar's breakfast; or through the Hispanic Theological Initiative; or the resources offered by the Foundation for Theological Exploration; or InterVarsity's the Well ministry (a fellowship group for women in the academy).

(looking around and seeing the experience of others), friendship (caring for others), aid (helping others), and advocacy (using whatever resources at your disposal to support and champion others). This doesn't mean that white men need to be left in the lurch. But when the reality of white normalcy sinks into our consciousness, the playing field is clearly not level. All inexperienced academics need mentorship, but there is an urgent need for mentorship, especially for those who have been marginalized.

DEAR WHITE AND/OR MALE COLLEAGUES

You may have read this chapter and had several different thoughts. One might be, *wow, I never knew, but I'm sorry for any way I have contributed to this.* Another thought might be, *what? This can't be true.* Or perhaps, *this sounds like what I have gone through as a disabled person; or when I spent time in another culture or overseas.* Maybe you are also wondering, *what can I do to help? How can I be a part of a new era of global and inclusive scholarship and academic cooperation?* Please allow me to offer the following advice.

Seek Understanding

Spend time being a quiet learner. I would recommend reading a book like *The Myth of Equality: Uncovering the Roots of Injustice and Privilege* (by Ken Wytsma). Sit down with people who are not like you and listen to their stories. Often, we assume we know why others are upset or frustrated with inequality issues, but we don't actually know their tales.

Make a Friend

When I was teaching at Seattle Pacific University, I regularly invited into my classrooms a representative from the John Perkins Center for Reconciliation, Leadership Training, and Community Development. He would share with students, not only about the life and legacy of John Perkins, but this one key piece of advice: *dare to form real friendships with people who are not like you.* This goes beyond having a conversation. Or even eating a meal together on the rare occasion. This requires time and commitment.

Awkwardness (at first). Even courage. But it is really the only way forward to a deeply transformed academy.

Advocate for Others

If you know your privilege (whether you are white, male, wealthy, etc.), I encourage you to look around and see how others might be experiencing marginalization or neglect. Most people are not looking for a handout, but rather respect and the opportunity to prove themselves. I feel very fortunate to be at a place in my career where I get asked to write for many projects. Some of these I am able to do, and others I have to say no. But I have made it a habit to refer the asker to one of my female and/or non-white colleagues. That is not because I don't respect my white/male colleagues. I partner with them all of the time. Rather, often projects come together through connections and relationships, and it is clear that women and people of color struggle to make those connections in the same way as their white male colleagues. So, I encourage you to be an advocate. This is not about reverse discrimination, unfair special treatment, or sacrificing quality—there are many incredibly talented female scholars and scholars of color. Rather, it is about recognizing the often-invisible imbalances that exist in the academy, and striving to be part of the solution; it is about paying sideways and forward the benefits we have, and patiently drawing attention to blind spots in our guild.

Conclusion

The previous chapters have endeavored to provide a series of responses to a host of questions that one may encounter when traveling down the path towards a PhD in biblical studies and beyond. Certainly you will stumble upon many more issues than could be discussed here. Thus, I leave you with a set of principles to keep in mind as further decisions come along and challenges appear.

- *Think Big Picture.* At any given point, the road may seem too difficult, and giving up may be the most enticing thing to do. It is here where I would encourage you to reflect on your sense of calling (as in "vocation"). As a Christian, you might feel that God has put you on this path for a reason. If you are not particularly religious, you still need to reckon with the matter of whether or not a life in the academic world (whether as a professor or in another segment of academia) will ultimately bring you fulfillment. I know that thinking about that future time of teaching and researching got me through many difficult seasons. At the same time, not everyone is cut out for the academic world. There should be no shame in realizing that. A PhD can only do so much good if the career choice is not the right fit.

- *Have a Support System.* It is in the DNA of many students to hole themselves up in the library for days on end, hunker down in a coffee shop with only books and an iPhone, and dodge people left and right in an attempt to make a deadline. At the end of the day, though, we all need friends and family that can help us decompress, process, and remember the world outside the sacred doors of the college. There will be times of frustration and failure where you will need a hug or sympathetic ear. You will want and need affirmation to press on after negative feedback. And, you will want people to celebrate with you in times of accomplishment and success. It is wise to take regular breaks from your work to spend time with these supporters and friends. Have non-academic hobbies, continue to participate in church or clubs, and take time to exercise and have fun with others. I benefited everyday from leaving my desk at about 4:30 p.m. and spending time with my wife and kids—I even cooked dinner most evenings! If such regular respites are not a part of your life, then that negative feedback from your supervisor or frustrating session in the library could easily send you wallowing in your failure.

- *Be Patient.* At many stages, whether before the PhD, during, or after, the opportunities to jump ahead or cut corners may be nearly irresistible. However, it shouldn't take my convincing to show you that there is nothing worse than looking back on your own work in disappointment because you took the easy road and did a sloppy job. Spend that extra week. Take that additional year. Work in such a way that you can be proud that you did all that you could to make your piece of research cogent and thorough.

- *Be Creative and Take Risks.* Let's be honest. Almost everyone who applies for a PhD program is smart. So who gets the acceptance letter? My guess is that it is those select few who are smart *and* creative risk-takers. Don't simply blend into the sea of academic faces. Think big, dream big, and do something bold and creative once in a while. There is a fine line, though, between creative risk-taking and arrogance. You must be careful that while you carry out your research, you show a spirit of generosity and humility, especially when interacting with the work of others.

- *Be Focused.* In many situations, whether in the PhD program or as a professor, you are given freedom to set up your own schedule of research and daily routine of work. Thus, you are left to set the pace of your work. It is very easy to lose the sense of urgency when you are setting your own deadlines! However, I suggest, especially during the PhD, that you learn to set reasonable deadlines for smaller pieces of your work, and do your best to stick to them. Now, there is no reason to be a slave to your schedule, especially in unique and trying circumstances; but, in general, the best PhD students are focused and disciplined when it comes to staying on target. They know how and when to say no and can differentiate between necessary divergences and those that are too far off track.

- *Be Eclectic.* Many PhD students and young professionals become a one-trick pony because their research was *so* focused that they are unaware of what is going on in the wider fields of biblical studies. While it is altogether appropriate and desirable to be an expert in one specific area, there is no reason that this has to become a permanent case of "tunnel vision." I would encourage you to maintain, alongside your primary specialty, an interest in a few other areas. This will actually enhance your research (as you gain insights from other fields), open up conversations at conferences, and could enhance employability.

- *Set a Benchmark.* When I had started my PhD program, I acquired the CVs of a few professors that I highly admire. I had set out to try and succeed in my PhD and early career looking at the standard that these fine scholars had set. Whenever I was tempted to lower my standards or cut corners, it helped to have these quality marks set in my head.

- *Count Your Blessings.* I will end on one of the best pieces of advice I think you may need to hear on the long journey through a PhD: *Remember the privileges of what you are doing.* In broader perspective, only a small percent of the world's population will have the chance (and honor) to study at the master's level, let alone spend several years at an even higher level in libraries and lecture halls in dialogue about important ideas. In those smaller moments of failure and difficulty, I encourage you to remember the blessing it is to have done the kinds of things you have done and to have the resources and support to participate in the privileges of higher education.

I hope this guidebook has been of some help to you in your journey and has aided you in preparing for your education and career. I wish you great success!

Bibliography

Aasgaard, Reidar. *My Beloved Brothers and Sisters! Christian Siblingship in the Apostle Paul*. London: T. & T. Clark, 2004.

Aland, Barbara, ed. *The UBS Greek New Testament: A Reader's Edition*. Peabody: Hendrickson, 2009.

Arnold, Bill T., and Brian Beyer, eds. *Readings from the Ancient Near East: Primary Sources for Old Testament Study*. Grand Rapids: Baker, 2002.

The Association of Theological Schools. "Transitions: 2017 Annual Report." https://www.ats.edu/uploads/resources/publications-presentations/documents/2017-Annual-Report.pdf.

Austin, J. L. *How to Do Things with Words*. Cambridge: Harvard University Press, 1962.

Bain, Ken. *What the Best College Teachers Do*. Cambridge: Harvard University Press, 2004.

Baird, William. *History of New Testament Research*. Vol. 1, *From Deism to Tübingen*. Minneapolis: Fortress, 1992.

———. *History of New Testament Research*. Vol. 2, *From Jonathan Edwards to Rudolf Bultmann*. Minneapolis: Fortress, 2002.

Baker, David W., and Bill T. Arnold, eds. *The Face of Old Testament Studies*. Grand Rapids: Baker, 1999.

Barrett, C. K. *New Testament Background: Selected Documents*. Rev. and exp. ed. San Francisco: HarperOne, 1995.

Ben Zvi, Ehud, et al. *Readings in Biblical Hebrew: An Intermediate Textbook*. New Haven: Yale University Press, 1993.

Berger, Peter L., and Thomas Luckmann. *The Social Construction of Reality*. New York: Doubleday, 1966.

Bird, Michael F. "Lynn Cohick on the Double Edged Sword of Being a Female Bible Scholar." *Evangelion*, October 19, 2013. https://www.patheos.com/blogs/euangelion/2013/10/lynn-cohick-on-the-double-edged-sword-of-being-a-female-bible-scholar/.

Bockmuehl, Markus. *Seeing the Word: Refocusing New Testament Study*. Studies in Theological Interpretation. Grand Rapids: Baker Academic, 2006.

Bond, Helen. "Helen Bond on Sexism and NT Leadership." *The Jesus Blog*, December 10, 2014. http://historicaljesusresearch.blogspot.com/2014/12/helen-bond-on-sexism-and-nt-scholarship.html.

Carson, D. A. Review of *Judgment and Justification in Early Judaism and the Apostle Paul*, by Chris VanLandingham. *Review of Biblical Literature* (2007). www.bookreviews.org/pdf/5679_6710.pdf.

Carter, Warren. *The Roman Empire and the New Testament: An Essential Guide*. Nashville: Abingdon, 2006.

Chapman, Steven B. and Marvin A. Sweeney, ed. *The Cambridge Companion to the Hebrew Bible/Old Testament*. Cambridge: Cambridge University Press, 2016.

Collins, John F. *A Primer of Ecclesiastical Latin*. Washington, DC: Catholic University of America Press, 1985.

Decker, Rodney J. *Koine Greek Reader*. Grand Rapids: Kregel, 2007.

Desrosiers, Gilbert. *Introduction to Revelation: A Pathway to Interpretation*. London: T. & T. Clark, 2005.

Douglas, Mary. *Purity and Danger*. London: Routledge & Kegan Paul, 1966.

Dunn, James D. G., and Scot McKnight, eds. *The Historical Jesus in Recent Research*. Winona Lake: Eisenbrauns, 2005.

"Eerdmans Statement on Three New Testament Commentaries." https://www.eerdmans. com/Pages/Item/59043/Commentary-Statement.aspx.

Ehrenberg, Ronald G., et al. "Inside the Black Box of Doctoral Education: What Program Characteristics Influence Doctoral Students' Attrition and Graduation Probabilities?" *Educational Evaluation and Policy Analysis* 29.2 (2007) 134–50.

Elwell, Walter A., and Robert W. Yarbrough, eds. *Readings from the First-Century World: Primary Sources for New Testament Study*. Grand Rapids: Baker, 1998.

Engberg-Pedersen, Troels, ed. *Paul in His Hellenistic Context*. London: T. & T. Clark, 2004.

Enns, Peter. *Poetry and Wisdom*. IBR Bibliographies 3. Grand Rapids: Baker Academic, 1997.

Evans, Craig A., and Stanley E. Porter, eds. *Dictionary of New Testament Background*. Downers Grove: InterVarsity, 2000.

Fee, Gordon D. *New Testament Exegesis*. Louisville: Westminster John Knox, 2002.

Filene, Peter. *The Joy of Teaching*. Chapel Hill: University of North Carolina Press, 2005.

A Foundation for Theological Education. "About the Fellowship." http://aftesite.org/the-john-wesley-fellowship/about-the-fellowship/.

Gasman, Marybeth. "An Ivy League Professor on Why Colleges Don't Hire More Faculty of Color: 'We Don't Want Them.'" Washington Post, September 26, 2016. https:// www.washingtonpost.com/news/grade-point/wp/2016/09/26/an-ivy-league-professor-on-why-colleges-dont-hire-more-faculty-of-color-we-dont-want-them/?noredirect=on&utm_term=.339ff991d228.

Geertz, Clifford. *The Interpretation of Cultures: Selected Essays*. New York: Basic Books, 1973.

Given, Mark D. *Paul Unbound: Other Perspectives on the Apostle*. Peabody: Hendrickson, 2009.

Gooder, Paula. *Pentateuch: A Story of Beginnings*. T. & T. Clark Approaches to Biblical Studies. London: T. & T. Clark, 2005.

———. *Searching for Meaning*. Louisville: Westminster John Knox, 2008.

Gorman, Michael J. *Elements of Biblical Exegesis: A Basic Guide for Students and Ministers*. Rev. and exp. ed. Peabody: Hendrickson, 2009.

Gorman, Michael J., ed. *Scripture and Its Interpretation: A Global, Ecumenical Introduction to the Bible*. Grand Rapids: Baker, 2017.

Gray, Patrick. ed. *The Cambridge Companion to the New Testament*. Cambridge: Cambridge University Press, forthcoming.

Green, Joel B., ed. *Hearing the New Testament: Strategies for Interpretation*. 2nd ed. Grand Rapids: Eerdmans, 2010.

Green, Joel B., and Michael C. McKeever. *Luke-Acts and New Testament Historiography.* IBR Bibliographies 8. Grand Rapids: Baker Academic, 1994.

Gundry, R. H. Sōma *in Biblical Theology: With Emphasis on Pauline Anthropology.* Society for New Testament Studies Monograph Series 29. Cambridge: Cambridge University Press, 1976.

Gundry, Stanley N. "Statement from Zondervan Academic on Dr. Andreas Köstenberger's John Commentary." https://zondervanacademic.com/blog/statement-from-zondervan-academic-on-dr-andreas-kostenbergers-john-commentary/.

Gupta, Nijay K. *1-2 Thessalonians.* Zondervan Critical Introduction to the New Testament. Grand Rapids: Zondervan, forthcoming.

———. *Beyond Belief.* Grand Rapids: Eerdmans, forthcoming.

———. *Worship That Makes Sense to Paul: A New Approach to the Theology and Ethics of Paul's Cultic Metaphors.* Beihefte zur Zeitschrift für die neutestamentliche Wissenschaft und die Kunde der älteren Kirche 175. Berlin: De Gruyter, 2010.

Gupta, Nijay K., and Jonah M. Sandford, ed. *Intermediate Biblical Greek Reader: Galatians and Related Texts.* Newberg, OR: Pennington, 2018. http://digitalcommons.georgefox.edu/pennington_epress/2/.

Gupta, Nijay K., and Scot McKnight, ed. *The State of New Testament Studies.* Grand Rapids: Baker, forthcoming.

Hauser, Alan J., and Duane F. Watson, eds. *A History of Biblical Interpretation.* Vol. 1, *The Ancient Period.* Grand Rapids: Eerdmans, 2003.

Hauser, Alan J., et al., eds. *A History of Biblical Interpretation.* Vol. 2, *The Medieval through the Reformation Periods.* Grand Rapids: Eerdmans, 2009.

Hausman, Scott. "An Announcement from Lexham Press Regarding EEC James." https://lexham-press.squarespace.com/blog/2016/9/19/an-announcement-from-lexham-press-regarding-eec-james.

Hays, Richard B. *Echoes of Scripture in the Letters of Paul.* New Haven: Yale University Press, 1989.

Hollander, John. *The Figure of Echo: A Mode of Allusion in Milton and After.* Berkeley: University of California Press, 1981.

Holmes, Michael W. *The Apostolic Fathers: Greek Texts and English Translations.* Grand Rapids: Baker Academic, 2007.

Horrell, David G. *Introduction to the Study of Paul.* 2nd ed. T. & T. Clark Approaches to Biblical Studies. London: T. & T. Clark, 2006.

Hostetter, Edwin C. *Old Testament Introduction.* IBR Bibliographies 11. Grand Rapids: Baker Academic, 1995.

Hunter, Alistair G. *Introduction to the Psalms.* T. & T. Clark Approaches to Biblical Studies. London: T. & T. Clark, 2008.

Jeffers, James S. *The Greco-Roman World of the New Testament Era: Exploring the Background of Christianity.* Downers Grove: InterVarsity, 1999.

Korb, Richard Alan. *Jannach's German for Reading Knowledge.* 6th ed. Boston: Heinle Cengage Learning, 2009.

Lakoff, George, and Mark Turner. *Metaphors We Live By.* Chicago: University of Chicago Press, 1980.

Lurie, Karen. *Crash Course for the GRE: The Last-Minute Guide to Scoring High.* 2nd ed. New York: Princeton Review, 2003.

Marsh, Clive, and Steve Moyise. *Jesus and the Gospels.* 2nd ed. T. & T. Clark Approaches to Biblical Studies. London: T. & T. Clark, 2006.

Mathewson, David L., and Elodie Ballantine Emig. *Intermediate Greek Grammar: Syntax for Studying in the New Testament*. Grand Rapids: Baker, 2016.

McEntire, Mark. "Why I Still Write Book Reviews." http://www.sbl-site.org/publications/article.aspx?ArticleId=311.

McKim, Donald, ed. *Dictionary of Major Biblical Interpreters*. Downers Grove: IVP Academic, 2007.

McNight, Scot, and Grant R. Osborne, eds. *The Face of New Testament Studies: A Survey of Recent Research*. Grand Rapids: Baker, 2004.

McNight, Scot, and Matthew C. Williams. *The Synoptic Gospels: An Annotated Bibliography*. IBR Bibliographies 6. Grand Rapids: Baker Academic, 2000.

Meeks, Wayne A., and John T. Fitzgerald, eds. *The Writings of St. Paul*. 2nd ed. New York: Norton, 2007.

Mills, Mary E. *Joshua to Kings: History, Story, Theology*. T. & T. Clark Approaches to Biblical Studies. London: T. & T. Clark, 2006.

Moyise, Steve. *Old Testament in the New: An Introduction*. T. & T. Clark Approaches to Biblical Studies. London: T. & T. Clark, 2004.

Neill, Steven, and Tom Wright. *The Interpretation of the New Testament 1861–1986*. Oxford: Oxford University Press, 1988.

Nickelsburg, George W. E. *Jewish Literature between the Bible and the Mishnah*. 2nd ed. Minneapolis: Fortress, 2005.

Phillips, Estelle, and Derek Salman Pugh. *How to Get a PhD: A Handbook for Students and Their Supervisors*. 2nd ed. Philadelphia: Open University Press, 1994.

Porter, Stanley E. *Handbook to the Exegesis of the New Testament*. New Testament Tools and Studies 25. Leiden: Brill, 1997.

Porter, Stanley E., and Lee M. McDonald. *New Testament Introduction*. IBR Bibliographies 12. Grand Rapids: Baker Academic, 1996.

Princeton Theological Seminary. "PhD Studies." http://www.ptsem.edu/academics/phd/program.

Reno, R. R. "A 2009 Ranking of Graduate Programs in Theology." *First Things*, October 2, 2009. http://www.firstthings.com/onthesquare/2009/10/a-2009-ranking-of-graduate-programs-in-theology.

———. "A 2012 Ranking of Graduate Programs in Theology." *First Things*, November 26, 2012. https://www.firstthings.com/web-exclusives/2012/11/ranking-theology-programs.

———. "Reno: Best Schools for Theology." *First Things*, August 30, 2006. http://www.firstthings.com/onthesquare/2006/08/reno-best-schools-for-theology.

Research Excellency Framework. "What Is the REF?" http://www.ref.ac.uk/about/whatref/.

Roncace, Mark, and Patrick Gray, eds. *Teaching the Bible: Practical Strategies for Classroom Instruction*. Atlanta: Society of Biblical Literature, 2005.

———. *Teaching the Bible through Popular Culture and the Arts*. Atlanta: Society of Biblical Literature, 2007.

Rosner, Brian S. *Paul, Scripture, and Ethics: A Study of 1 Corinthians 5–7*. Leiden: Brill, 1994.

Sampley, J Paul, ed. *Paul in the Greco-Roman World*. 2nd ed. London: T & T Clark, 2016.

Sandberg, Karl C., and Eddison C. Tatham. *French for Reading*. 4th ed. Englewood Cliffs: Prentice Hall, 1997.

Sandy, D. Brent, and Daniel M. O'Hare. *Prophecy and Apocalyptic: An Annotated Bibliography*. IBR Bibliographies 4. Grand Rapids: Baker Academic, 2007.

Schweitzer, Albert. *The Quest of the Historical Jesus*. Minneapolis: Fortress, 2000.

Scott, James C. *Domination and the Arts of Resistance: Hidden Transcripts*. New Haven: Yale University Press, 1990.

Seifrid, Mark A., and Randall K. J. Tan. *The Pauline Writings: An Annotated Bibliography*. IBR Bibliographies 9. Grand Rapids: Baker Academic, 2002.

Shillington, V. G. *Introduction to the Study of Luke-Acts*. T. & T. Clark Approaches to Biblical Studies. London: T. & T. Clark, 2007.

Sørensen, Bent Meier. "Let's Ban PowerPoint in Lectures: It Makes Students More Stupid and Professors More Boring." *Independent*, February 24, 2017. https://www.independent.co.uk/news/education/lets-ban-powerpoint-in-lectures-it-makes-students-more-stupid-and-professors-more-boring-a7597506.html.

Sparks, Kenton L. *The Pentateuch: An Annotated Bibliography*. IBR Bibliographies 1. Grand Rapids: Baker Academic, 2002.

Stuart, Douglas K. *Old Testament Exegesis: A Handbook for Students and Pastors*. 4th ed. Louisville: Westminster John Knox, 2009.

Temporini, Hildegard, and Wolfgang Haase. *Aufstieg und Niedergang der römischen Welt*. Berlin: De Gruyter, 1972–.

Tucker, Ruth. "12 Year Update." https://www.ruthtucker.net/.

Vance, Donald R. *A Hebrew Reader for Ruth*. Peabody: Hendrickson, 1993.

Van der Watt, Jan. *Introduction to the Johannine Gospel and Letters*. T. & T. Clark Approaches to Biblical Studies. London: T. & T. Clark, 2008.

Vanhoozer, Kevin J. *Biblical Narrative in the Philosophy of Paul Ricoeur: A Study in Hermeneutics and Theology*. Cambridge: Cambridge University Press, 2007.

Wallace, Daniel B. *Greek Grammar beyond the Basics: An Exegetical Syntax of the New Testament*. Grand Rapids: Zondervan, 1997.

Watson, Francis, ed. *The Open Text: New Directions for Biblical Studies?* London: SCM, 1993.

Weeks, Stuart. *An Introduction to the Study of Wisdom Literature*. T. & T. Clark Approaches to Biblical Studies. London: T. & T. Clark, 2010.

Westerholm, Stephen, ed. *The Blackwell Companion to Paul*. West Sussex, UK: Wiley-Blackwell, 2011.

"What's Your Speech Rate?" http://www.write-out-loud.com/speech-rate.html.

Wheelock, Frederic M. *Wheelock's Latin*. Edited by Richard A. LaFleur. 5th ed. New York: Harper, 1995.

Whitacre, Rodney A. *A Patristic Greek Reader*. Peabody: Hendrickson, 2007.

Wilson, April. *German Quickly: A Grammar for Reading German*. Rev. ed. New York: Lang, 2004.

Wytsma, Ken. *The Myth of Equality: Uncovering the Roots of Injustice and Privilege*. Downers Grove: InterVarsity, 2017.

Ziefle, Helmut W. *A Modern Theological German: A Reader and Dictionary*. Grand Rapids: Baker, 1997.